THANATOPICS

A Manual of Structured Learning Experiences for Death Education

J. Eugene Knott
Mary C. Ribar
Betty M. Duson
Marc R. King

Single copies of this publication may be pur-
chased for $12.50 plus $1.50 for handling and
postage from: SLE Publications, P.O. Box 52,
Kingston, RI 02881.

Library of Congress Catalog Card No.: 81-85149

Knott, J. Eugene et al
     Thanatopics: A Manual of Structured Learn-
ing Experiences for Death Education.

Kingston, RI: SLE Publications

111 p.

8201   811021

ISBN   0-9608230-0-X

Printing   5   4   3   2

Contents

Acknowledgements

Significant contributions "behind the scenes" were made by several people in order to get this book in print. We wish to recognize especially Russell Kolton, Jo-Ann Lepore and Barbara Haney for giving the content a form, and Earl Knott for literal support. Also, we wish to express our gratitude to the contributors of exercises and ideas for *Thanatopics*, as well as a few thousand of our (collective) students over the years, who have provided the "laboratory" in which these SLEs have been tried, refined, and renewed many times over. Their teaching has suffused our learning through SLEs.

Also, we thankfully acknowledge the following reprint permissions:

Laura Huxley, *You Are Not the Target.* New York: Farrar, Strauss, and Giroux, 1963, for "Attending Your Own Funeral."

Robert Kastenbaum, in Datan, N. and Ginsberg, L. (Eds.). *Life-Span Developmental Psychology: Normative Crises and Interventions.* New York: Academic Press, 1976 for "Pecking Order of Death"

Peter Passell, *How To . . .* New York: Farrar, Strauss, and Giroux, 1976, for "Longevity Calculation."

Salten, Felix (Estate), *Bambi.* New York: Simon and Schuster, 1956, for Chapter 8 (pp. 72-75) excerpt.

Introduction

Woody Allen (1976) once quipped, "I'm not afraid to die — I just don't want to be there when it happens." Of course we must be there when our own death occurs, and the prospect frightens many of us. But in growing numbers, young and old alike are no longer willing to keep death a closet topic — off limits to social discussion and even personal inspection. Once an area laden with taboos, death now is confronted more routinely through the mass media as well as through death education courses that reach students in public, private and professional schools, universities and adult education classes.

Rationale

By its very nature, our own death and the deaths of those we love involve us personally. Can death education then be so designed to involve personally the participant learners? We believe so. Schulz (1978) describes death education as serving basically two purposes: "It can make the final phase of life more predictable and controllable, and it can give the individual the opportunity to understand his emotions about death and dying." Yet a third by-product of death education is the enhanced understanding and control that the individual comes to feel toward their life and living as well as toward their dying and death. Such objectives as these are not readily gained through the mere dispensation of information, for they encompass one's personal values, self-image, life goals, coping styles, relationships, and philosophy about the quality of life and living. Accordingly, one of the assumptions underlying the approach of this book is that affective responses to death-related issues are as important as merely cognitive ones.

In a recent review of the published research on the effects of death education, Oshman (1978) summarized the picture thus:

... virtually all of the studies which have demonstrated effectiveness have employed programs which ... have included elements of an experiential and more personally involving nature such as taped or live interaction with a dying patient, group process discussions, or explicit focusing on personal feelings about death. Further, in all of the studies which report negative findings, these more personal or experiential elements were absent (p. 11).

In calling this an apparently essential experiential base, he goes on to say, "This suggests that it may be necessary to combine didactic formats with more experiential ones within programs of death education to effectively alter attitudes toward death or reduce death anxiety."

A book of structured learning experiences for the death educator seems long overdue, as thousands of educators in dozens of fields — health and medical, social sciences, literature, funerary and so on are engaged in teaching about the many nuances of life in the 1980's lived in the face of the modern day milieux of mortality. Further, while there are scores of books and a growing number of articles, (particularly in *Death Education*, and less often in *Omega* and *Essence*) which speak to pedagogical concerns in thanatology, little exists to assist the teacher methodologically in this regard. In fact, to our knowledge, only a handful of books are available which speak to this purpose, and they are often overly specified or narrowly focused in ways that this manual is not. For instance, *Discussing Death* by Mills, et al. (1976) is an excellent compendium of lessons or units geared to grades 1-12, and covers a wide swath of thematic objectives. Two other paperbacks: *Death Out of the Closet* by Stanford and Perry (1976), and *We Are But a Moment's Sunlight* by Adler, Stanford, and Adler (1976) are both useful sourcebooks involving collections of diverse writings that, in the former are like Mills, et al. in approach to curriculum, and in the latter, provide varied anthology of readings. Again, both are a bit different in form, content and target readership from the present effort. Neale's *The Art of Dying* (1971) and Worden & Proctor's *PDA* (1976), a pair of helpful personalized approaches to death education, are early examples of the inclusion of self-survey types of structure used in the context of information-sharing, but both of these are a bit dated now and are out of print. More recent publications, such as Simpson's *Facts of Death* (1979) and Bugen's *Death and Dying: Theory, Research and Practice,* (1979) differ from the present book in that they are general in address, survey a broad set of topics, offer some structured aids to the instructor and student, but only the latter samples any structured learning exercises. In summary then, it appears that the field has evolved to a place where significant need has created demand for a collection of materials such as the following pages offer.

Thanatopics is arranged in a highly usable form, emphasizing the "intact" character of each exercise, and yet organized into a handful of sections with internal consistency and thematic relatedness. Further, the 50 exercises are written in a fashion that comprehensively speaks to the integrity of the total learning experience, not to a discrete, simplistic stimulus-response format which can "abuse" learner, topic, and instructor alike. All SLEs herein, are multiply tested and "later generation" revisions.

Purpose

With the goal of integrating the aforementioned cognitive and affective learning dimensions, this book is designed to provide educators and learners with a variety of structured exercises and organized discussion activities that will assist them in examining and integrating the often confused or elusive feelings and attitudes people have toward death.

We see this book as a highly complementary resource for death educators of all stripes, but particularly those from middle school through higher and professional education, and agency, community and religious educators dealing with the topics represented herein. The formats described are particularly adaptable to those, and to similarly structured learning settings.

Further Rationale

There are additional reasons which support this structured experiential approach to death education beyond that already cited:

1. Most people need structure to assist them in exploring and discussing death-related issues.

Such structure offers both encouragement and relative safety to examine feelings and thoughts which normally are defended against by an individual left to his or her solitary devices. This would appear to be so especially in this era of Westernized living, wherein death for most is "once removed" from frequent personal acquaintance by the institutionalization of dying. Adding to this effect is the buffering or insulating from reality that portrayals of death in modern media often promote when they emphasize solely the sensational aspects. Research on the use of structure in group activities supports the kind of approach promoted herein, as Lee and Bednar (1977) note in citing the effects on both individual members and the group as a whole:

"... structure tends to reduce group participant personal responsibility for behavior in early group sessions, thereby increasing the potential for high risk-taking behavior and the development of group cohesion in later group sessions (p. 191)."

Developmentally speaking, the elements of adaptation to loss and mortality appear in infancy, usually become understood more complexly with each passing year into adulthood, and undergo alteration as new data and experiences are taken in until one's death. The capability for making personal sense of these can be enhanced by having a supportive, open climate for integrating the new data as one grows. Then too, the earlier in the developmental schema this process occurs, the more likely it is that one can succesively use each as a building block. Being able to do so without the uncomfortable, sometimes painful feelings that dying and death evoke when they occur unexpectedly is a true advantage to an experiential death education approach — throughout life ideally.

2. Effective education is tied closely to the interpersonal context in which it occurs.

New learning experiences are often enriched when integrated through constructive interaction with others. This seems particularly relevant to a topic like death which is, as Kastenbaum (1977) notes, definable in as many ways as there are settings in which and people to whom it occurs. By exposing oneself simultaneously to multiple inputs from others and to one's own inner thoughts and feelings about personal mortality and loss, there often occurs a mutually facilitative process of combined subjective and objective learning.

In an excellent discussion of many of the issues of importance in experiential group education, Marks and Davis (1975) point out well the merits of the experiential approach over a merely didactic one. They compare the former to participating in a lively discussion while the latter contrasts sharply as listening to a one-way lecture. The differences are drawn between the two, particularly on the issues of *involvement* and *responsibility.* In the experiential model one becomes involved in the process of active learning while the didactic is limited to activity on the part of the lecturer, aside from any intellectual stimulation possibly gained. They go on to argue that the entire frame of reference one assumes in experiential learning is more learner-centered, and can incorporate greater numbers economically, while expanding the potential diversity of inputs. In sum, they point out that such a model is more complete, allowing for personal points of reference, both cognitive and affective inputs as well as interchanges, and incorporation of theoretical or conceptual material. Generally, the transfer of learning beyond the intitial experience is found to be greater and more consistent as well.

3. Learning about death is a lifelong process that does not end with a death education "course" any more than it truly begins there for most.

Experiential education within the aforementioned group context also maximizes the likelihood of such continued learning throughout one's developmental passages. This can occur through the early removal of blocks to exploration, teaching a *process* of searching, and by modeling the value of plain, direct talk about death and dying, their implications and meanings. Developmental researchers have argued that the experience of loss and life-threatening implications are part of the human legacy, and occur from birth onward. As one matures and life changes are experienced, including losses of significant others, the perspective one acquires with each transitional shift brings with it a concurrent alteration in viewpoint and even behavioral change, as the specter of mortality is enhanced and becomes increasingly personal in its implications. Bugental (1973-4) a leader in the humanistic movement within psychology was one of the earliest proponents of this goal and means, when he advocated structured group exercises as a productive way of enabling one to confront the existential meanings of personal death. While our first and most common "lessons" in death education are usually unstaged, natural occurrences, those who teach about these topics also must assist learners to integrate and crystallize the meanings of those changes and transitions. One certain and universal goal of death education is to foster recognition of Toynbee's observation that "... in the midst of life, we are (also) in death!"

Some Guidelines for Conducting SLEs

In this section, we will outline and describe some important points for consideration for leaders of SLEs. These are concerns which are relevant both to the implementation of previously structured experiences and to the design of any new ones. For a more comprehensive generic treatment of similar matter the reader is referred to Cooper and Harrison

(1976). First, we shall deal with some facilitator guidelines, and then take a look at some caveats that bear weighing in the overall use of SLEs.

Facilitation Issues

The role of leader in conducting a structured learning experience is one calling for more than simply doing things "step by step!" Facilitating a SLE is more complex than merely rendering a recipe. The facilitator must attend with equal skill to "what is done" as well as "how it comes about." Therein lies the ultimate responsibility, *and* the true process of learning in an experiential mode — to begin acquiring some new data about oneself as a result of having experienced some novel and personalized input.

Overall Schema

Marks and Davis (1975) have outlined a broad, five step model for facilitators which is highly useful as an overall schema for considering that which is essential and germane to conducting SLEs. They are:

Step 1 — *Preparation*
Step 2 — *Introduction*
Step 3 — *Activity*
Step 4 — *Debriefing*
Step 5 — *Summary*

We'll consider these steps a general guide as we look at some crucial points to address in the use of SLEs in death education. First, then, let's examine preparation issues.

Facilitator Functions

The following perspective on the responsibilities which accrue to the educator using SLEs may be of some assistance. Lieberman, Yalom and Miles (1973), writing in another context, have identified four basic functions of the group facilitator thus: *(1) Emotional stimulator:* especially in conducting SLEs and with the often emotive nature of death-related topics, the capacity to foster expression of feelings and personal attitudes, to be "evocative" in one's interaction with the participants is needed. It is a skill demanding balance, maturity, and comfort with the process, as too little personal involvement or too sensationalistic and too intense an approach will both yield a disappointing outcome, or worse, might result in some psychological damage; *(2) Caring:* This dimension of responsibility is to be taken literally. The participants are not merely "subjects" or impersonal "characters" in a play. SLEs are very much a human enterprise, usually with transactional activity at the center of the experience. No less than fully attentive, compassionate concern is demanded of the leader(s); *(3) Meaning attribution:* The ability to make beneficial, educative use of the SLE once it has begun is perhaps the most vital function of the four, as the learning "comes home" only with a skilled facilitator at this juncture. The capacity for enabling participants to analyze their own experience of the SLE and to make their own meanings out of it is most important. No small part of this is the need for insuring that each other's viewpoint is also seen and appreciated, particularly where variance and diversity occur; *(4) Executive function:* The last category of functional responsibility for group facilitators is essentially a "managerial" function. This includes possession of a working knowledge of what is entailed in all five steps of the leader model, and being able to execute them well with accurate timing, and to "debrief" the experiences as one goes along. Finally, responsibility for following up as needed is part of the complete duty of the group facilitator. More on this will be taken up later.

Conceptual Skills

Conyne (1975), in a look at the *prior* types of (conceptual) knowledge which the group facilitator should bring to the conduct of any SLE, cited a trio of points to ponder. He argues that the leader of any group first needs to know and understand *people;* i.e., one must have a thorough cognitive understanding of human functioning, including developmental and behavioral attributes and their manifestations. Second, a complete understanding of *groups;* i.e., being familiar with interpersonal behavior and the development of the group itself as a converging set of personalities is needed. The third — a knowledge of different *styles of group facilitation* — involves a talent for utilizing different ways to facilitate group movement (dynamics) through different phases of the experience.

Prerequisites for Facilitators

In other words, we would urge that the following five premises be taken as basic prerequisites for effective facilitation of SLEs. They are, in a nutshell, familiarity with ...

(1) the *topic* being addressed in the exercise;
(2) the *audience* being led through the SLE;
(3) the various elements of *group dynamics;*
(4) the specific *exercise* or *SLE* being used *before* application, preferably by having experienced it in some role; and
(5) the *resources* available for handling any "fallout" that the SLE may occasion.

This latter premise bears some expansion. This benchmark is a preparatory need which hopefully will not be implemented often. It seems inevitable, however, that over time, in using SLEs, an educator will encounter a situation where, unknowingly, a participant will be vulnerable to overidentification with a particular aspect of the experience. An example that comes to mind is the use of a role play situation wherein loss of a child through death is involved. Inadvertently, a member of the learning group or class may be a recently bereaved parent for whom the enactment may trigger some painful memories, thoughts, and feelings. Rarer still, but not unknown, is the person who warily comes to a death education course or workshop, and finds the matter of personal mortality or death loss too frightful emotionally. This seeming "thanatophobia" is an example of an emotional effect which the facilitator must contend with by helping the person cope in their own way with the feelings the SLE generates. Where it proves desirable to use other referral agents to deal with this so-called "fallout", that too is a requisite part of a thoroughgoing preparation. While it may not be necessary to implement this aspect of preparation, one should learn to anticipate the unplanned, to be adaptable to the unexpected.

Conducting the SLE

This prefatory section of comments regarding the use of SLEs in death education would be incomplete without some general remarks on the actual conduct of the groups, and thus we turn now to introducing and carrying out the activity.

Participation: At the outset of any SLE, each would-be participant should be made fully aware that the level of personal involvement must be decided by each individual. While risk-taking might be encouraged by the leader or instructor, no one should feel coerced in any way into participation. By modeling such acceptance and flexibility, the facilitator is a key figure in establishing the kind of open and permissive atmosphere that legitimizes voluntary participation.

Developmental Sequencing: Because of the nature and variety of the structured exercises presented in this manual, some will involve deeper levels of exploration and disclosure than do others. Then too, some SLEs are aimed intentionally at being introductory exercises, while others are only appropriate with a stable group of participants who have had some length of time to work together on less intense topics, and to build some cohesion. Lastly, these exercises are intended primarily for use with an adult learner, but most are readily adaptable to a younger population, including as young a learner group as junior high or middle school age students. It is recommended that the facilitators pay careful attention to the objectives and categorical type of each SLE in the attempt to provide experiences that are attuned to the readiness level of the participants.

Timing: The temporal "feet" on which SLEs move are really a pair. Timing itself is a matter of knowing what to use and when to achieve the desired educational result. This is the "pivot foot", so to speak. The other foot is the more mobile one, consisting mainly of a flexible length for using the SLE, with adequate time for debriefing and followup being the most important allowance.

Physical logistics: The location or setting wherein the SLE is conducted is an important feature to consider. Often, flexible seating is desired as subgroups are formed and reformed, and free movement is essential. Also, comfort in those surroundings is a key facet of the scenario, as too austere or intemperate an enviroment is too easily distracting, and compromises the impact of the SLE needlessly.

Another "physical" element involves the use of materials and media aids. Generally speaking, there are two basic thoughts to hold when utilizing such aids or any extensive number of tools in the completion of the SLE. First, complexity seems to be grasped best when it is symbolically simplified. A corollary thereto is that examples "tell" twice as well! However, one must always beware the overuse of such aids, particularly an overreliance on audiovisual tools. Careful planning and moderate use of materials in constructing and directing SLEs are definitely worthwhile parts of a good planning process.

One final point á propos physical logistics is embodied in a similar caution regarding the basic difference between active versus predominately passive SLEs. Remember that the connection between the neurons at the base of the spine (one's seat) and those in the brain where even passive presentations are ideally aimed is distant, lengthy and indirect at best. The active learner is usually provided a true advantage!

Processing and debriefing: An essential component of the experiential learning process involves the exploration and discussion of participants' reactions to the exercises. Facilitators should insure adequate time for talking about the feelings, thoughts, and actions that are generated by a particular structured experience. By talking about the experience, participants can be assisted in clarifying, refining, and elaborating their learnings so that both appropriate generalizations and personal messages might be extracted from a given design.

Since the impact of exercises such as those offered in this book occasionally is delayed, and reactions to the experience might not emerge until an individual has left the setting, it is important for the instructor to remain available to participants at other times, between meetings when feasible or to provide for someone to be available as needed. It is also helpful to encourage participants to write down between sessions any thoughts and feelings that occur to them if the SLEs are part of an ongoing program. Journals or reaction papers of this nature provide participants with an additional means of integrating their experiences, as well as offering the instructor ultimate access to how the experiences are affecting each individual. An interesting variant of this is to pair or team students for this type of ongoing dialogue, possibly including provision for a jointly submitted final summary statement.

Several additional guidelines are suggested for assuring optimal impact of the debriefing procedure: (1) While respecting each individual's right to the privacy of his or her own reactions, it is important to obtain some understanding of how the experience affected the different participants; (2) discovery of interaction patterns and the evolution of group cohesiveness can be facilitated through the discussion of commonalities of experience, while (3) individual differences in response to the exercises are to be valued. It is important to suspend judgement of individuals' observations and feelings, and to legitimize a variety of reactions to and realizations about the experience. Learnings that the experience was designed to reveal may be underscored effectively throughout the debriefing process by referring to the goals intended occasionally.

This segment began as a series of caveats for the conduct of structured learning experiences in death education. Our experience with SLEs leads us to regard them as potentially very powerful interventions and teaching tools. We strongly encourage that they be utilized only with appropriate care by experienced death educators and group facilitators. In summary, the ageless maxim about good communication has particular application here as one implements SLEs. Simply, one should begin by always introducing what one is going to do, then do so, and finally, summarize all that has been done during the exercise and as a result of debriefing.

Completion of SLEs: Also, like any other intervention, SLEs demand evaluation of their overall effects on learners, including (pardon the pun) any "postmortem" analyses that are required to determine the reasons why, on occasion, use of a SLE failed to produce the desired or expected result. A comprehensive evaluation includes participant feedback both immediately and after the passage of some time, as well as the utilization of observer critique where feasible. Although difficult to do directly, more empirical applications of measures of outcome and effectiveness should be devised and employed whenever possible. Most of the SLEs to follow are latter generation versions, improved after much trial and experimentation, and following such evaluations of the uses of each.

Innovation

Further, it is important that the outlines of these structured experiences be viewed as somewhat general guidelines, or suggestions to be tried. The need to experiment, innovate and personalize is in no context greater than in this type of educational methodology and with this general topic. What is presented here are merely sets of central ideas with the structural latticework for further application and elaboration provided. As noted earlier, these SLEs are a compilation of second and third generation revisions of original exercises, and are the products of several peoples' labors. Where known, we have given credit to the originator, and have secured reprint permission wherever called for, particularly of copyrighted material. We have not knowingly failed to cite an outside author, even when the final product represents a radical revision of their germinative idea. More than two-thirds of the SLEs that follow were devised by one or more of the present collaborators. We are already in receipt of a handful of exercises for sharing in a possible second volume, and would welcome submissions by any students or educators so inclined.

Learner Responsibility

SLEs basically build on personal inference, or an active and directive "inductive" learning paradigm, as opposed to the basically "deductive" or logical application utilized with more impersonal bodies of knowledge. As Middleman and Goldberg (1972) once wrote of structured experiential learning,

The importance of the here-and-now, of action and reaction in the living moment, as a potent dynamic in the learning process is widely accepted. There is general agreement that knowing *which derives from direct experience is significantly different from* knowing about *which the more vicarious, didactic methods yield (p. 203).*

In such, the responsibility for learning rests within the participant/learner, and endorses the belief that personal change is preceded by acquisition of new experience or learning, including both externally validatable evidence as well as internally acknowledgeable "facts".

Augmenting the SLE

The use of lecturettes to support, extend, or translate from personal symbolism to generalizeable application beyond oneself is an important means of augmenting SLEs. Conceptual material in combination with experiential learning molds a process of education which enables one, as the old Indian aphorism admonishes" ... (to) walk in my brother's shoes", (in order) more fully to understand his perspective, feelings, understandings and beliefs.

Finally, while the outcomes of structured group based learning are sometimes therapeutic experiences, that end is clearly secondary, as the structure itself is intended to promote an educational character, not one of therapy *per se.*

There are over 65 hours of activities in the next four sections. Some of the uses and advantages of selected specific exercises or combinations of SLEs in *Thanatopics* include:

- ability to choose a SLE to fit the particular tenor of the "class"
- selection from several related topically appropriate SLEs
- clearly spelled out goals for each exercise
- a common format enabling both student and facilitator to use several SLEs and to draw comparisons via format, time-frame, materials, variations, debriefing objectives, evaluation analysis.
- explicit narrative suggestions which are offered where desirable throughout, enabling more facile adaptation by the leader
- a thoroughly readable style with easily referenced titles and goals in an uncomplicated categorization.

Categories of SLEs

Each of the structured experiences in the book is grouped into one of four major categories for comparison and for purposes of handy reference. The categories are listed below with a brief amplification of the type of material to be found in each. This system is totally of our choosing, and the reader will be stimulated (we hope) to improve on it and to expand the usage of each idea to other applications in death education.

1. Introductory, Warm-ups, Ice-breakers. Fairly superficial in their impact, these are, as stated, literally intended to help broach the topic at hand, and to offer a fairly high degree of psychological safety. They often are used early in the life of a group, course, workshop, or program.

2. Values Clarification, Affective Experiences. Sid Simon once stated that death issues provided the ultimate values clarification experience. This category contains some reasonably intense, self-disclosing SLEs whose purpose is to illuminate one's personal posture toward some aspect of human mortality or the consequences thereto. They should not be employed in an initial meeting nor with a group unfamiliar with each other, but preferably after some previous common discussion of theme and a bit of interpersonal sharing has been accomplished.

3. Instrumental Exercise and Applied Designs. This presents a short collection of "forms", some newly devised and others generally available in like format. All require a paper and pencil involvement, usually beginning individually, with interaction only after partial or full completion of the form.

4. Role Plays. This section is a series of vignettes designed to elicit new perspectives through enactment of a role. While fairly limitless in the ways one might devise for their use, not everyone is able readily to glean new viewpoints from portrayals, as not all people role-play equally well. This can be a very dynamic mode of learning, but care in directing and skillful debriefing make or break the impact here.

Format of SLEs

This section provides a listing and short explanation of each component of the SLE format commonly used within the following compendium of exercises. They appear in the order outlined. Where a component is omitted, it is missing due solely to its exceptional lack of relevance to the particular SLE being described.

Title — the label given as a working description of the SLE's overall topic of focus

Goals — the broad objectives of the total experience as presently conceived

Setting — any particular environmental attributes encouraged for conduct of the SLE

Materials — literally what tangible tools and quantities of them are called for to complete the exercise

Time — the overall minimum required to conduct the SLE as given

Procedures — a step-by-step outline of each part of the SLE, including leader notes where applicable

Variations — alternative ideas for using similar approaches to achieve comparable results; procedural options

Debriefing — suggestions for framing the process of inquiry into the effects of the experience on the participants; the "processing" phase which completes each SLE

References — where appropriate, literary references for direct usage, or for supplemental information usable at the discretion of the leader

References

Adler, C. S., Stanford, G., and Adler, S. M. *We are but a Moment's Sunlight.* New York: Washington Square Press, 1976.

Allen, W. *Without Feathers.* New York: Warner, 1976, 106.

Bugen, L. A. *Death and Dying: Theory, Research, and Practice.* Dubuque, IA: William C. Brown Co., 1979.

Bugental, J. F. T. "Confronting the existential meaning of my 'death' through group exercises." *Interpersonal Development.* 1973-74, *4*, 148-163.

Conyne, R. "Training components for group facilitators." In Pfeiffer, J. W. and Jones, J. J. (Eds.). *The 1975 annual handbook for group facilitators.* LaJolla, CA: University Associates Publ., 1975, 138-140.

Cooper, C. L. and Harrison, K. "Designing and facilitating group activities: Variables and issues." In Pfeiffer, J. W. and Jones, J. J. (Eds.), *The 1976 annual handbook for group facilitators.* LaJolla, CA: University Associates Publ., 1976, 157-167.

Kastenbaum, R. *Death, Society and Human Experience.* St. Louis: Mosby, 1978, Chapters 1-5.

Lee, F. and Bednar, R. L. "Effects of group structure, and risk-taking disposition on group behavior, attitudes and atmosphere." *Journal of counseling psychology,* 1977, *24*, 191-199.

Lieberman, M. A., Yalom, I. D., and Miles, B. B. *Encounter Groups: First facts.* New York: Basic Books, 1973.

Marks, S. E. and Davis, W. L. "The experiential learning model and its application to large groups." In Pfeiffer, J. W. and Jones, J. J. (Eds.). *The 1975 annual handbook for group facilitators.* LaJolla, CA: University Associates Publ., 1975, 161-166.

Middleman, R. R. and Goldberg, G. "The concept of structure in experiential learning." In Pfeiffer, J. W. and Jones, J. J. (Eds.). *The 1972 annual handbook for group facilitators.* LaJolla, CA: University Associates Publ., 1972, 203-210.

Mills, G., Reisler, R., Robinson, A., and Vermilye, G. *Discussing Death.* Palm Springs, CA: ETC Publ., 1976.

Neale, R. E. *The Art of Dying.* New York: Harper and Row, 1971.

Oshman, H. P. "Death education: An evaluation of programs and techniques." *Journal supplement abstract service,* 1978, *8*, 18 pp.

Schulz, R. *The Psychology of Death, Dying and Bereavement.* Springfield, MA: Addison-Wesley, 1978, 169.

Simpson, M. *The Facts of Death.* Englewood Cliffs, NJ: Prentice-Hall, 1979.

Stanford, G. and Perry, D. *Death Out of the Closet: A curriculum guide to living with dying.* New York: Learning Ventures/Bantam, 1976.

Worden, J. W. and Proctor, W. *PDA: Personal Death Awareness.* Englewood Cliffs, NJ: Prentice-Hall, 1976.

I. Introductory, Warm-Ups, Ice-Breakers

In this first section, a number of initial SLEs which could serve as "ice-breakers" in a group are presented. They each can serve as fairly uncomplicated, relatively unthreatening introductions to the general topic of death by enabling participants to engage in a brief examination of some aspect of the place of mortality in current thought or experience.

These include structured experiences with historical, developmental, or sociocultural frames of reference. Their use is most clearly recommended in early, introductory phases of a death education program or course.

1. Bones

Goals

To examine causes of death and attitudes toward death as revealed by examining skeletal remains. A number of professionals are engaged in examining bones to determine, not only cause(s) of death, but also a number of other things about the person. Participants will gain factual information on bone study as well as knowledge about the inferences which can be made about the life and life style of the person whose bones are being examined. Students will have a tactile experience with a dead person and an opportunity to explore the attitudes of persons whose jobs require contact with bones of dead persons.

Materials

Professional expert on bone study (possible sources: museum, coroner's office, anthropology department, medical school).

Time 40 minutes.

Procedures

Speaker should give overview of work, and in his/her presentation pass around skeletal samples. During the presentation the speaker should explain the process used to determine age, cause of death, life circumstances, sex, and nutritional history from skeletal remains. The samples should illustrate specific findings (i.e. skull, pelvis, leg bones for age, nutrition, cause of death, sex). If possible have the speaker develop a more extensive personal history of a person whose skeletal remains are being examined (i.e. family background, cause of death, circumstances by which the bones were secured for study). Questions and discussion should follow. Obviously, one will need to have access to specimens and to someone with expertise in this area. Handling bones is optional. Local museum or college personnel may be good sources.

Debriefing

1. Did you know that so much information could be gained from skeletal remains?
2. How did you feel about handling the bones at first?
3. How did you feel as they became more personalized?
4. Did this presentation show respect or disrespect for the body?
5. What attitudes toward life/death did the speaker have?
6. Did this presentation have any effect on your attitudes toward life/death?

2. Book Watch*

Goals

To identify own and others' responses to death-titled books.

Materials

Books with death or death-related titles — usually course-related books.

Time

Single session 30-40 minutes with 4 to 5 days between assignment and session.

Procedures

Assign participants/students to carry textbooks or other books which have Death and Dying in the title for a period of 4 to 5 days. Take these books with you everywhere such as shopping, riding the bus, meetings, etc.

Observe people's responses to your literature, and you. Record the verbal and nonverbal responses which occur. The fact that there may be nonverbal responses is as important as verbal ones.

Unless absolutely necessary, do not volunteer the information that this is for a course in death and dying. At the conclusion of your interaction, if verbal with someone, participant tells why he or she is carrying these books. After revealing this information observe any change in the relationship, tension, etc.. If so, note how.

Have participants write a minimum of two pages and a maximum of six pages relating to the following information.

a. Describe the variety of responses which occurred.
b. What response was most prevalent?
c. Substantiate that the responses reflected the attitude that death is denied in this society or that death is accepted as a part of life in society.
d. Do these general responses of others reflect your basic responses to death? If so, how? If not, why?
e. How comfortable or uncomfortable did you feel carrying out this assignment? Attempt to analyze the reason(s) for feeling the way you did.

Have students share paper with one another.

Debriefing

1. How were your experiences similar? different? What do you see as reasons for similarities or differences?
2. In what way was the exercise useful as an introduction to this course?
3. What difficulties did you have writing your paper?
4. Would you change this exercise in any way to achieve the same results?

---

*Suggested by Pat Hess, San Francisco, CA.

3. Childhood Recollections of Death and Dying

Goals

1. To increase awareness of how personal attitudes about death and dying develop.
2. To identify how one's present attitudes and feelings toward death and dying relate to early experience.
3. To discover the extent to which one's feelings about death and dying are shared by others.

When people are able to discuss and explore together their personal experiences and feelings about death, they can often discover that their attitudes about death and dying are shared by others. In order to explore fully one's feelings about death, a structure for exploration is often necessary.

Insofar as childhood memories are reflections of the past, exploring and discussing such memories about death and dying can be less threatening than directly discussing one's current feelings. Through the process of exploration, participants are often able to generate memories and feelings which they had previously forgotten. These early experiences can then be reviewed to determine how they might be currently influencing one's attitudes about death.

Materials

Poster paper or blackboard on which to write discussion questions.

Time   Minimum of one hour

Procedures

1. Instruct participants to form small groups of three to five members. Have each small group find a comfortable location in the room.

2. Introduce the exercise: "This activity is designed to assist us in remembering and talking about our childhood memories and experiences of death and dying. One of the purposes is to increase our awareness of how we felt about death as a child. This awareness may then help us understand our present feelings and assist us in clarifying what attitudes we might wish to change."

   "You may find that you can't remember many experiences. You may also discover that someone else's memories remind you of a variety of experiences you had forgotten about."

   "You may also find that there are some experiences you prefer not to discuss with your group. That is perfectly OK. Talk about only what you wish to talk about."

3. The leader then introduces the first topic of discussion. Because some groups might require more time to discuss certain topics, the leader might allow flexibility by writing the topic headings on the blackboard and encouraging each group to move through the topics at a pace that is comfortable to each. Then they are told to review in their mind's eye and share as they are willing and comfortable.

   "What were some of your earliest experiences with death when you were a child? Was it a death of a person? A pet? What feelings do you recall about these experiences? Who did you go to talk to about your feelings?"

   PAUSE

14

"How did members of your family deal with their feelings about death and dying? What particular memories do you have about how your family expressed their feelings?"

PAUSE

"What did you learn about death from your peers and close friends?"

PAUSE

"What are your memories of times when you were responsible for killing some living thing? What feelings did you have about these experiences? What feelings do you now have about these experiences?"

PAUSE

"What are your early memories of times when you thought you were going to die or be killed? What feelings did you have about these events? Who did you turn to for help?"

Debriefing

Suggested questions to be discussed among the entire group as a way of achieving closure for the activity:

1. What have you learned about your attitudes toward death through this exercise? How do you feel about this experience?
2. What other questions might we have discussed about our childhood memories of death?
3. What might be done to assist children in exploring their attitudes and feelings about death?

References

Grollman, Earl A., *Talking About Death: A dialogue between parent and child*, Boston: Beacon Press, 1970.

4.   Daily Headlines

Goals

1.   To expand awareness of number of everyday events associated with death and dying.
2.   To increase understanding of how media influences our attitudes about death and dying.
3.   To assist in developing sensitivity and empathy for those who have experienced a death of a loved one.
4.   To promote discussion about kinds of personal and social needs of individuals who have recently experienced the death of a loved one.

Everyday, newspapers and other media present us with objective accounts of death experiences. Eventually, we become desensitized to these accounts. As Stalin once observed, "A single death is a tragedy, while a million deaths is a statistic." This exercise is designed to assist participants in developing sensitivity to some of the human issues involved for those who experience the loss of a loved one.

Setting

Room large enough for participants to spread out reading materials and interact without disturbing others.

Materials

A current issue of a major daily newspaper, a pencil, and a felt-tipped pen plus a blank sheet of paper for *each* participant.

Time   Minimum of 1 hour.

Procedures

The Leader distributes a newspaper and a blank sheet of paper to each participant. He tells each participant to scan the newspaper looking for ten different articles that describe some event that involves the death of a person. The Leader instructs the participants to mark these articles with a felt-tipped pen.

The Leader then instructs each participant to select one of the articles to examine in detail, giving the following instructions:

"The article you selected describes the objective, measurable fact of some person's death. Imagine you are able to step inside the people who are intimately involved with the story and rewrite it, describing how you believe each person might really feel about the death if each were able to fully verbalize it: 1. Describe how the dead person himself/herself might have felt about his/her own death, 2. Describe how his/her loved ones might feel about the death of the person they loved. Take your time and describe as fully as you can all the feelings you think these people might experience.

The facilitator might allow enough time for each participant to write and describe the feelings of at least 2-3 people involved that are affected by the death experience. They then instruct the participants to sit in a close circle and each participant is invited to read aloud: 1. the original newspaper account of the death, and 2. their own written account that describes the feelings of the deceased and his/her loved ones. They might be encouraged to read the written description slowly and with sensitivity.

Variations

Another strategy which has merit in this exercise is that suggested by Robert Kastenbaum in his course at the University of Massachusetts. He has the students use scissors rather than markers and they cut out à la swiss cheese, not only obits, but *any* ad or article or picture which is even remotely mindful of death in some manner.

Debriefing

After each participant has had an opportunity to read their written story some of the following group discussion questions might be asked:

1. What was this experience like for you?
2. What was it like for you to try to imagine and describe how a dead person might have felt about his/her own death? How his loved ones might feel about his death?
3. What was it like to listen to these accounts of some person's death? Did this experience stir up any feelings you might have about the deaths of people you have loved? If so, what were some of the feelings?
4. What kinds of assistance do you imagine loved ones might need to help them deal emotionally with the death of the person they loved?
5. What are some of the ways that mass media influences our attitudes and feelings about death? What kind of constructive changes might be suggested?

5. Death Collage

Goals

To have participants identify pictures and words which they associate with death and life, and to examine why they associate such symbols with one or the other. Also to examine the interrelationships and/or distinctions made between life and death.

Materials

Work space, many magazines, scissors, glue, backing paper, large envelopes.

Time Two 40 minute sessions or 1.5 hours.

Procedures

Session one: Explain to the participants that they will be making individual collages which will have to do with life/death. Allow participants 30-40 minutes to go through magazines and cut out as many pictures and words having to do with life and death as possible and put them in their large envelope. Participants will take envelopes with them at the end of the session. Between sessions, if this is done in two sessions, participants are encouraged to look over pictures and words and add to them. Instruct them not to discard any items at this time. Session two: At the beginning of this session have participants find a work space and arrange items, discards may be made at this time, and glue them onto a backing to make a collage. No further instructions should be given. Allow 15-20 minutes for this activity. At the end of this time assemble all participants with their collages. Have each participant explain his/her collage, answer questions, and then display the collages. Discuss activity.

Debriefing

1. What kinds of things did you choose to represent life? death? Were they similar or different?
2. When you looked at them between sessions did you have any difficulty identifying which ones were death and which ones were life?
3. Did you add any words or pictures between sessions?
4. Which group of items was easier to assemble? Why?
5. Were you more aware of possible inclusions between sessions than you were before you began this exercise?
6. When you began to construct your collage did you mix or separate life and death items?
7. Are they part of one another or separate and distinct?
8. Did you communicate with anyone about this project — either in the group or outside the group?
9. Did anyone help you or did you help anyone else? Why or why not? Who?
10. Did you have any difficulty with any part of this activity?
11. Did the choosing of pictures and words, the putting them together and the explaining of your collage give you any perspective or insight into your own attitudes toward life and/or death?
12. Did you discard any items? If so what items and why? If not, why not?

6. Death is Funny!*

Goals

1. To provide a medium for exploring societal views and treatments of death.
2. To look at some ways death is dealt with in song.
3. To initiate discussion about the taboo nature of death in some subcultures.
4. To provide some examples of death-related humor.

Early in the life of a group or class, it is often worthwhile to examine how death falls on our consciousness socially in various ways. One way of injecting some vitality into this process is by looking at how death has been portrayed in song and humor. This also enables us to look at the salutary benefits of "laughing" at the things which pose a threat to living.

Materials

Phonograph or tape player and recordings of the numbers below. There are numerous discographies published too, which cite more contemporary recordings available, and while not predominantly humorous, more and more lyrics of late are reflective at death themes.

Time

Variable; allow about 20 minutes to play a sufficient variety of themes, then another 20 or so minutes to debrief.

Procedures

Begin by introducing the topic generally, noting that we often use humor to relieve tension or to avoid anxiety-provoking thoughts and conversation with "taboo" areas such as sexuality and death. Emphasize that this is not altogether a bad idea. In fact, being able to see the humorous side of distasteful events has frequently been humankind's saving grace! It is an essential dimension in helping define the breadth of human nature.

Examples of humorous recordings poking fun at death's specter could include:
- Bill Cosby on "Rigor Mortis" (from his record "I Started Out as a Child")
- "Pore Jud Is Daid" from Oklahoma!
- "The Funeral Tango" from Jacques Brel Is Alive and Well (etc.)
- Mark Twain's story about "Accident Insurance" (from Hal Holbrook's album, Mark Twain Tonight, Vol. II)
- Tom Lehrer's song "We Will All Go Together When We Go" (from his album, An Evening Wasted with Tom Lehrer)

Variations

Sometimes, if the group seems really interested in the possibilities of this topic, they can be divided into small groups to make group collages expressing themes like "death and humor" or "American attitudes toward death." For this, stacks of newspapers and magazines along with scissors, paste, poster board, etc. can be provided. The final products can be posted and described for the whole group to engage in discussion. Or, an annotated list can be made and updated for sharing.

Debriefing

Lyrics such as those cited above lend reference in different ways to cultural attitudes, postures toward death, dying, and mortality. Many of them harken back to a previous period,

*Suggested by Joan McNeil, Manhattan, Kansas.

while more recent tunes usually make more contemporary statements about our collective belief system and values. Suggested lines of questioning which can be pursued include:

1. What made the humor evident in each situation?
2. How much is fantasy a factor in these tunes?
3. What do these lyrics have to say about immortality? Aren't these recordings themselves paeans to the immortal heritage of their creators and performers?
4. What taboos are expressed in the lyrics?
5. How has cultural evolution affected our views of the sentiments expressed in these songs?
6. Did you find certain things especially humorous? Which and why? Others, not funny to you? How so?

7. Ethnographic Interviews

Goals

To examine various customs related to death, funerals and burial and explore the cultural attitudes and attendant rituals through interviews with a variety of people.

Materials

Paper, pen/pencils, markers, large sheets of newsprint, tape.

Time   Three 40-minute sessions.

Procedure

First Session: Have participants break into groups of four or five. Groups should decide what aspects of death, funeral and burial they will investigate as a group, where they will locate the population to be interviewed and the number of interviews to be conducted — each member should do at least ten interviews. Individuals could be interviewed as well as representatives of death-related businesses — florists, funeral directors, clergy, cemetery personnel, obituary writers, musicians, printers, casket makers. ... At this session the group should also determine the interview format, questions and individual responsibilities of group members. If group members have never done interviews before, this would be a good time to give interview guidelines and practice with one another.

Second Session: This session should be at least a week after the first session to allow enough time for all interviews to be completed. During this session group members should compile interview findings and make generalizations or draw conclusions from their findings. They should also prepare visual materials or handouts for presentation to the whole group at the third session.

Third Session: At this time each group will present findings and explain its interview process, population and how it arrived at its conclusions or generalizations. The total group will then compare findings and identify, either areas of support or conflict, and attempt to make some general observations about death, funeral and burial rituals based on interview findings. At this point group members may wish to share any interesting individual encounters while interviewing. Discussion should follow.

Variations

A.*   In groups of 4 to 6, have participants construct a questionnaire on death which will be used to interview students, teachers, parents, and members of the community. The questionnaire should attempt to find out how society has an impact on values and attitudes toward death. Each group should contact at least 20 people or five interviews per participant. Allow one week for construction of questionnaire, interviews and tallying of results.

The questions on the questionnaire can serve as a guide for inquiry into society's view toward death and life. After sharing results, have participants write their own perspective toward death and share this with others. Discussion follows.*

B.**   Each participant will interview three to four different people about their personal experiences with a death in their family. The participants should attempt to interview people of different age, sex, occupation, marital status, religion, and ethnic backgrounds. In talking with these individuals, participants should try to learn the following: (1) How has the individual experienced death in his/her family — how many, who, when, where, what circumstances, type of death? (2) Was there any one death in the family that was especially significant to the individual? (3) What were the initial and prolonged reactions of the individual and of the family to the death? What initial and long-range effect did the death have on the individual? on the family? (4) Did the individual and the family go through a period of mourning? Were there any special rituals or activities following the death?

Following the interviews, either in a paper or discussion, participants should (1) Define crises and identify whether the death identified by the individual was a crisis for the individual and/or the family; (2) Compare and contrast the grief and mourning responses of the interviewees. Using theory from readings on grief and grief reaction to establish criteria for normal and abnormal grief, identify if these responses were normal or abnormal grief reactions. Substantiate the type of grief with data from the interviews; (3) Discuss reactions and difficulties encountered in talking with individuals interviewed. If no difficulties were encountered, discuss why there were none.**

Debriefing

1. How did you determine who you would interview?
2. What did you want to find out in your interviews?
3. Why did you think that your specific population would help you find this out?
4. How did you decide what questions to ask?
5. What happened when you approached people? What was their response to the topic? to you? How would you have responded?
6. What did you find to be unique about the population you interviewed?
7. Were your results what you thought they would be?
8. Were there areas of agreement? of conflict?
9. Was there any note of difference between past and current practices?
10. How did you feel asking questions about death?
11. Did you find out anything about your own practices in relation to the population interviewed?
12. What influence does society or family have on attitudes and practices at time of death?

---

*A. Suggested by John A. Bonaguro, Ohio University, Athens, Ohio.
**B. Suggested by Pat Hess, San Francisco State University, San Francisco, CA.

8. The Funeral*

Goals

To observe, attend, and reflect upon institutionalized practices related to funeral services.

Materials   Newspapers; recent, preferably.

Time   One week between assignment and group session.

Procedures

Have participants look up a funeral in the "Funeral Notices" in the newspaper and select a funeral to be held at a church or mortuary or synagogue or temple which is at a time convenient for them to attend.
Attend a memorial service which provides an opportunity to observe various institutionalized practices.

After the funeral, have participants write a brief report of their observations and personal reactions to it. (Attach the obituary notice of the funeral attended.) *The report should be a minimum of three pages with a maximum of ten pages, typed.*

Special Instructions:

1. It will be helpful, before you attend the funeral, or immediately after, if you are unfamiliar with the religious affiliation of the person whose funeral you attended, to find further information about the religious practices related to death.
2. Include the obituary notice with your report.
3. *No more than* two participants are to go to any one funeral.
4. If two participants attend a funeral together, each MUST submit a separate paper.
5. Papers should include properly documented theory.
6. *Each paper should include the following:*
    a.   What social purposes of the funeral were evident in this particular funeral? Give examples for each social purpose.
    b.   What were the particular religious, social, and cultural rituals for grieving in the funeral service? What purpose did they seem to serve?
    c.   What particular social values were in evidence at this funeral?
    d.   Briefly describe the behavioral responses toward death and/or grieving of those attending and those officiating at the funeral. Upon what attitudes might these behavioral responses be based?
    e.   In what way did the funeral seem to assist the bereaved with the grieving process? In what way did it seem to interfere with the grieving process?
    f.   Briefly describe your reactions and feelings at the funeral. Attempt to discover the basis for these feelings and reactions.
    g.   Have participants share papers at the beginning of the next session.

Debriefing

1. What did you hear that was new to your experiences of institutionalized practices related to death? What was familiar?
2. Was there any aspect which was especially appealing or unappealing to you?
3. In what ways are institutionalized practices particularly responsive or unresponsive to human or social needs?
4. Would you do this again? Why or why not?
5. What changes would you make in institutionalized practices? Why or why not?

*Suggested by Pat Hess, San Francisco, CA.

9.   Growing Up with Death*

Goals

1. To sensitize participants to the developmental nature of the concept of death (i.e. children's reactions and understandings are different than adults.)
2. To enable students to relate to the unique needs of children of various developmental stages.
3. To provide a supportive environment in which participants can examine their own childhood experiences with death.

Materials

See references below for sources of children's stories.

Time   Varies; at least one hour, preferable two.

Procedures

Each participant should select and read a children's story with a death theme before the session. During the session, s/he will tell the story in summary and discuss the developmental level, appropriateness, theme and whatever seems interesting to them about the story.

A small group format, with 6-8 members is ideal, but this can be done in a large group. In that case, the instructor might select representative literature and assign it to a few students for reading and presentation.

Debriefing

1. Why do you think you selected the story you read?
2. Does it present death as irreversible? Universal?
3. What do you remember related to death that happened during your childhood? At what age?
4. Discussion can also bring out stories and games that illustrate a childhood belief that death is reversible and not universal (Sleeping Beauty, Ring-A-Rosey, Little Red Riding Hood, Chicken, Peek-A-Boo, etc.).

References

Participants can read Chapter I from *The Child and Death*, Hostler, L. "The Development of the Child's Concept of Death" (Ed. O. J. Sahler, M.D.), Mosby, 1978. This book has an excellent bibliography from which books and stories can be chosen for reading.

They might also be referred to Grollman, E. A., *Talking About Death*. Boston: Beacon Press, Rev. 1976, for more reference and stories.

---

*Suggested by Susan Woolsey, Baltimore, Maryland.

10. I'm Coming Back As ...

Goals

1. To provide an introduction to some aspects of belief in reincarnation.
2. To introduce a new group of students to one another (ice breaker).
3. To give opportunity to a death education class to clarify some values of living *and* dying.

Materials

This can be conducted with or without writing responses down, but seems most easily accomplished with pencil and paper for each participant.

Time

About 5 minutes per participant plus another 10-20 minutes for summary discussion.

Procedures

This SLE serves as a "light" way to get into the topic of death and beliefs about immortality. It can be introduced simply as a fun way to creatively project how we might "return"/"reincarnate" if we could come back after our deaths as someone or something else. It should also be stated that such fantasies often reveal some of our values and impressions of unfulfilled wishes and lifestyle variations.

Distribute paper and pencil/pen and instruct the group members thus:

a. "I want you to let your mind, your imagination go to freely connect with some thoughts and images you've not had before. Imagine that you could have your choice of returning to 'live' or 'be' in this world in a new form of existence after you died."

b. "I'm going to suggest several categories to help frame your thoughts, but other than that, you should just let yourself go to picture what reincarnated form you might wish to take. We're going to do this for about 3-4 different categories, and I'll give you a couple minutes for each."

c. "You're to state first the answer to the question and then write down under that on your paper what prompted you to select that response, what appeals about that reincarnated form."

d. "First, *if* you could come back as a *color*, what would that color be? ... Once you've chosen that color and written it down, directly under it, state briefly why you made that choice — be creative but be yourself in doing so."

e. The facilitator instructs the group similarly for a couple more categories. Those that have been fruitfully used in the past were "machine, flower, bush, plant or tree, day of the week, small animal, large animal, type of automobile, historical person, currently living person, etc."

f. Choose only about three or four as time is needed to share the answers and rationales later. It also seems helpful to proffer the categories in somewhat of a hierarchy, going from inanimate to animate things, and increasing the complexity as you go.

Debriefing

Questions can be dealt with either as a whole group or in sub-groups of four or more if the class is large.

1. How did you feel about this exercise?

2. Do you have strong feelings about "reincarnation" in some form?
3. Which of those you wrote (or some other) is fondest to you?
4. Do any of your choices reflect some unrealized wishes, some regrets or fantasies unfulfilled about your life as it has been?
5. What have you learned during this, about the elements of your lifestyle you cherish?
6. If important people in your life had the same "choices", would you want them to "come back" as something or someone compatible or quite different? Why?
7. Have you given this or any other notion of immortality some thought before? If yes, what was the outcome?

11. Journal*

Goals

To provide an opportunity for ongoing personal reflection and writing. To identify patterns, puzzles, questions, answers, ideas, feelings, and resources. To record and perhaps share growth, change, self-knowledge, new learning, and old learnings newly discovered. To provide facilitator with a regular, informal, non-threatening means of communication and feedback from and with individuals in an ongoing group.

Materials   A notebook, diary or blank book for each person.

Time

At least 30 minutes between sessions. Could be short daily entries or one or more longer entries weekly.

Procedures

Have participants record reflections about each session between sessions. These journals should have no format requirements and should allow participant to write freely about the group experience as well as any feelings, insights, observations, questions, answers, new learnings, new insights into old learnings, and any other related topic.

Journals should be read regularly by facilitator with any needed follow-up noted. It is often helpful for the facilitator to write answers, comments, reflections to writer. The journals should remain a confidential and individual form of communication between participant and facilitator.

Debriefing

1. This would take place regularly through reading, writing, and comments.
2. At the end of the group sessions the following would be a useful form of debriefing.
3. Was the journal helpful?
4. Was it easy or difficult? How so?
5. What would you change or do differently?
6. Were comments helpful or would you prefer no comments?
7. What types of entries did you make most often?
8. Did you share anything in your journal with others in the group? Outside the group? If so, what prompted this sharing? What was the response? Would you do it again?
9. Will you continue to keep a journal? Why or why not?

Variations

Journal entries can be shared with other group members at the beginning of each session on a voluntary basis, or, group members can form dyads and share journals with one another at some point in each session.

---

*Suggested by Pat Hess, San Francisco, CA.

12.   The Mayflower

Goals

To provide an emotional context and insight into an historical event or series of events with moribund features.

Setting   Room with a large open space.

Materials

Facilitator may want to be familiar with several accounts of Pilgrim/Puritan history and journey of the Mayflower as well as diary accounts of the first year in the New World.

Time   30-45 minutes.

Procedures

Facilitator should have all participants (save one member to be held out at beginning) assemble at one corner of the room. When all are gathered standing, the facilitator begins to provide the group with its identity and circumstances; thus:

"We are going to do some group role playing of a significant historical event. As I narrate the scenario, imagine yourself as a real member of this actual group. See if you can 'get into' it. Let's begin:"

"It is 1608 and you are in England. Due to religious differences with the government, you relocate to live in Holland. Most of you are craftspeople for whom work and social integration in the new home are not easily found."

"You weather those trials for over 10 years, until you grow weary of the difficulties of such a lifestyle, and, fearing that your children will lose all touch with their cultural heritage, you decide to go to the New World. There you hope to find better opportunities to preserve your culture and community, as well as less restriction on the expression of your religious values."

"So, on August 5, 1620, you have returned to Southhampton, England, and are embarking on such a journey aboard a pair of former wine carrying vessels, the Mayflower and the Speedwell." (Begin to move group slowly toward opposite side of room.).

"You're not even at sea for two weeks when the Speedwell begins to leak, and thus both ships return to England." (Move group back to original place.).

"Since the leak turns out not to be repairable, 102 people — 73 men and 29 women and children crowd onto the Mayflower and set sail again in early September." (Instruct the group to crowd very closely together.).

"Only 35 of the total are Pilgrims! Twenty-five are the ship's crew, and the rest are people being sent by an English company to start a new colony. The crossing is arduous!" (Begin moving group slowly across the room.). "Many are sick!" (Stop group and have them rock back and forth while holding their stomachs and foreheads.). "One man dies!" (Arbitrarily pick one (male) out of group and "retire" (him) from the group.). A short while later, a child is born (Have withheld person crowd into group.) and is named Oceanus. (Have group move over to opposite wall, and then back them up 5 steps, then forward — repeating this three times).

"Finally, after 66 days at sea, and after nearly another month wandering the coastline to find a suitable landing and settlement, it is December 26, 1620 and you are in the midst of winter in a foreign unsettled place. As you begin to erect homesites, the long journey, weather, and lack of agricultural know-how combine to take their toll of healthy settlers. You expected to live by fishing and fur trading but have no usable equipment. You know nothing of ice fishing, trapping and trading here, and you have no farming experience. Your heritage is not farming but crafts. In the first 2 months your collective 'catch' is one cod, three seals, and an eagle. You're exceedingly cold, hungry, and lonely. Sickness strikes and, within 3 months, half of you die, often at a rate of 2 or 3 each day." (At this point, either by pointing out or tapping half the members, "kill" 50% who are to leave the group and take seats.).

"Only 50 people of the original 102 are left. Not only do many die, but most of the living are too sick to work or even get around." (At this point, "tap" all but 1/7 — calculate in advance — of the group, instructing those picked out to sit or squat down where they are.).

"You who are well must bury the dead, care for the sick, and try to stay well and survive yourselves. In March, things begin to look up, as your leader, Miles Standish helps you befriend two native Americans, Samoset and Squanto, who speak some English. Squanto introduces you to Massasoit, the chief of the Wampanoags. You make several accords, and in the spring of 1621 the Indians teach you how to survive by being farmers. They show you, for instance, how to plant corn using fish for soil fertilizer, and your first crop comes in beautifully in mid-summer." (Have the standees pull the "sick" up to indicate a gradual return to health.).

"By autumn, your situation looks much better, and you decide to celebrate by holding a feast called 'Harvest Home.' It is based on celebrations you held in England. Governor Bradford, your elected leader, invites the Wampanoags to the feast, which goes on for three days. The Indians bring food along to share, and the menu consists of turkey, venison, duck, clams, corn, squash, wild fruits and berries, cornbread, ale, wine, and many other good foods."

"This first Thanksgiving was a playful time, with wrestling matches, marching drills, foot races, lacrosse, and other games played by all."

"In early 1622, another ship arrives, but when it returns to England, none of you sail on it! As the years went by, the idea of a Thanksgiving Day was taken up by some of the other colonies. In November of 1789, George Washington issues the first Presidential message saying we should have a day of thanks and commemoration. In 1863, President Abraham Lincoln proclaimed that a national Thanksgiving Day should be on a fixed Thursday in November. And today we know what that feast has come to be. Thus ends our historical trip."

Debriefing

1. What things bound you together as a community?
2. How was your trip?
3. What was your feeling when the first person in your group died? When the new child was born?
4. What were your feelings when you finally made it to the new land? When you found out what it was like?
5. How did you feel when so many people began to die? If you were one who stayed alive? If you were one who died?
6. How did you feel if you were a sick survivor? A well one?
7. What was your feeling in spring?
8. What feelings did you have for the community?
9. Was it worth it?
10. Why didn't anyone go back?

13. Media Survey

Goals

We are all exposed to multiple media deaths daily although we are rarely involved with the person or persons. In many ways, this exposure may contribute to forming general attitudes toward death and it often leaves people unprepared for the variety of feelings which accompany the personal experience of death and the mourning process. This experience attempts to make participants aware of "media death" and the attitudes and behaviors it fosters.

Materials

Paper, pencils, access to a TV set, TV schedule, overhead projector or blackboard.

Time Two sessions of 45-50 minutes each.

Procedures

First session: This session should include an introduction to "media death" and development of a schedule for viewing as well as a check sheet, or observation sheet to be used by all viewers. A schedule should be worked out to cover all channels and hours of programming, with specific groups or individuals responsible for viewing and recording observed data. After a schedule has been established, including commercials, previews and newsbreaks, etc. the group needs to determine a specific, common data collection sheet which specifies type of information to be gathered by all observers. This might include the following: program identification information, actual observed deaths, type, cause and circumstances of death, references to death, response of others, relationship of others, death vocabulary, funeral or memorial services, who is responsible for making the arrangements, if reference to them is omitted, disposal of the body, feelings described about the death or the person, social impact of the death, mourning process, were the deaths those of individuals identified by name or member of a group and identified by the group they belonged to, were any values expressed about either life or death. The group may wish to focus on a single aspect or to observe a variety of things. Each observation should include identification information such as channel, time of day, type of program or presentation, intended audience, length of program. At the end of the first session each participant should have specific viewing responsibilities and a common observation sheet to be completed before the second session. Participants may decide to work in groups or alone and an attempt should be made to cover at least one consecutive 24 hour period of programming.

Second session: The gathered data is compiled at this time using the observation sheet as a basis with provision for recording any additional observed data. Each observation is recorded in order to gain an overall picture of "media death". This should take 10 to 15 minutes.

After data is compiled the total group may be sub-divided into groups of three or four to examine findings and make generalizations or draw conclusions about "media death". This should take 10 to 15 minutes. At the end of this time each sub-group should share conclusions and total group may wish to determine a follow-up either individually or as a group.

Debriefing

1. Was your TV viewing any different from normal? Did you notice different things?
2. Was your recreational TV viewing affected by your observations?
3. Was death generally presented in a context?
4. Was it personalized?

5. What were the common causes of death?
6. In what ways were the deaths you observed similar or different from your experiences with death?
7. Is "media death" realistic? Should it be more or less realistic than it is?
8. How is death presented in children's programming? Daytime shows? News? Comedy? Drama?
9. What life values are expressed in the reporting of deaths?
10. Do you have any specific examples of a particularly good or bad presentation of death in the media?
11. In what ways could you communicate your opinion to those responsible for programming?
12. What program suggestions would you make about the presentation of death?

14. Mything Death

Goals

To have participants write, illustrate, and construct a book of original death myths.
To examine existing and original death myths.

Materials

Paper, construction, or drawing paper, pen/pencils, typewriter, crayons, markers, cardboard, magazines, tables, scissors, glue, copier, clasp folders, hole punch.

Time   Two 40-minute sessions.

Procedures

This exercise is designed to accompany a mythology lesson. After study of the origin, purpose, and use of myths, and some specific myths, participants will, either alone or in groups of not more than three, write a myth which explains some aspect of death. This session may take a full 40-minute session. If some participants finish before the time have them title, type and illustrate their myth. Encourage original drawings but allow the use of pictures cut from magazines.

Each participant should come to the second session with a titled, typed and illustrated myth. At the second session myths are read aloud and questions are answered by the author(s). The entire group then decides upon an order for their mythology book. All myths should be included.

One of two things can happen at this point; a single book can be constructed with small groups being responsible for various sections — cover design and construction, table of contents, author information, foreword, glossary, index, introduction, dedication, pagination and sequencing; or, if a copier is available copies of all myths can be made for each student. While copies are being made each student will design his/her own cover, table of contents, dedication, author information, etc. When copies are made each participant will put together his/her own book. Participants may then share those individually designed parts of their books.

Debriefing

1. Was it hard to think of a myth to explain death?
2. What symbols or symbolic persons did you choose for your myth? Why?
3. Why did you illustrate your myth in this particular way? Is there anything in your personal experience that helped you when you wrote?
4. What were the advantages/disadvantages of working in a group or alone?
5. How did you react when you heard and saw the other myths?
6. Why do you think the myths in this book were ordered in the way they were?
7. Why did you choose the dedication you did for this book?
8. Was it more difficult or easier to write the other parts of the book?
9. What attitude toward death is expressed in this book?
10. Is the book in general similar to or different from your attitude toward death?
11. To what audience would this book appeal — age, sex, background ...?
12. Can you think of a person you know to whom you might lend or give this book? Why?
13. Is the myth you wrote consistent with your view of death? Why/why not?

(**Note**   This can be used in conjunction with the study of mythology, history, creative writing, language study, art, anthropology, psychology or social studies.)

15. Patchwork*

Goals

To provide an indirect method of revealing attitudes toward life and death.

Materials

Swatches of different materials. Three or four matched sets of swatches with fifteen to twenty different fabrics including: bright, subdued, soft, coarse, useful, ornamental, small figured, large figured, striped, plaid, polka dot, dotted swiss, net, cotton, wool, denim, corduroy and velvet.

Time   1 to 1.5 hours.

Procedures

Participants are divided into groups of seven or eight. Each group is given a complete set of the fabric swatches and asked to spread them out so each person can see each piece. Each person is instructed to pick out the piece which most nearly identifies their personality traits. After they have made their selections, they tell the group about it. When everyone has had the opportunity to share, participants are instructed to select the materials they cannot identify with in any way. They again relate why they chose the fabric.

The first two activities help them see their personality traits as reflected in the fabrics and to explain the similarities and differences to other members in the group. The entire group gains information that help each participant become more aware of others.

In the third round the group selects the one fabric they could all "live" with. This is difficult to accomplish because it requires a consensus of opinion.

Next, the facilitator asks participants to think of all the swatches as making a patchwork quilt and each piece of the patchwork represents an individual participant. Each is different like the patches in a quilt; each having unique qualities, personalities, peculiarities, meaning and dimensions.

In an additional round, participants are asked to choose fabrics which represent or suggest a death or life theme and this is followed by a discussion of the colors and fabrics of life and/or death.

Debriefing

1.   Were any of your choices of fabrics in the early part of this exercise similar to the one you chose for life or death?
2.   Were choices at this point similar or different from one another?
3.   If you were making a quilt of these pieces would they be separate or mixed together in your quilt?
4.   Did anyone choose the same fabric to represent life and death?
5.   How interconnected are life and death?
6.   What did you find out about yourself or your attitudes during this exercise?
7.   What selection was the most difficult? The easiest? Why?
8.   If you were making a single quilt about life or death, what would it look like?

---

*Suggested by Richard Hause, Kansas State University.

II. Values Clarification, Affective Experiences

This longest section offers a range of introspective and variously intense experiences. All require at least a moderate amount of participant self-disclosure, and they focus on the many nuances of living in the shadow of death and often unavoidable dying, albeit influenced as to time of occurrence for many.

A thorough consideration of the group's readiness for delving into such material is warranted, and facilitators are urged to use these SLEs only after some period of initial acquaintance and interaction has been accomplished. Some of these are similar in a few respects to role-playing exercises, although the "roles" to be assumed in this section are personal and not to be acted.

16. Activities Contraction Brainstorm*

Goals

1. To acquaint individuals with the kinds of daily decisions faced by many terminally ill persons.
2. To sensitize individuals to the restricted activities available to those who are confined to bed with a terminal illness.
3. To serve as a stimulus for discussing various aspects of the dying process.

Through a brain-storming procedure participants are stimulated to identify the typical day-to-day activities and decisions the terminally ill must relinquish due to health, diminished mobility, and restricted resources.

Materials

On a large sheet of paper or on a blackboard, the Leader draws the following:

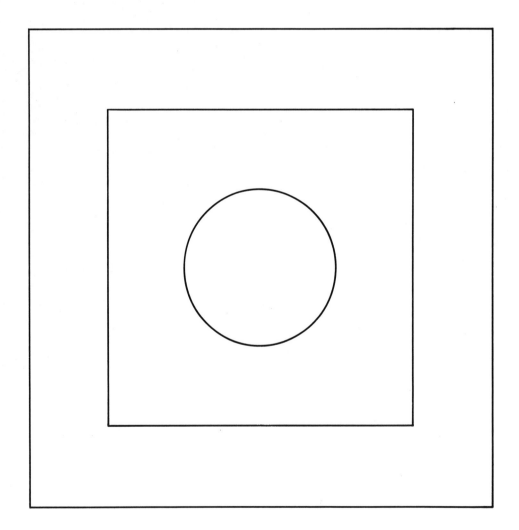

---

*Suggested by Dorothy Stanton and Panna Rothe, Toledo, Ohio.

Time One hour.

Procedures

The Leader requests participants to form a semi-circle of chairs around the blackboard. The Leader then explains:

1. "The outer square represents all activities you can do and decisions you can make on an average day when you are feeling totally rested and healthy. What I would like you to do is to think now of the sorts of things you would make and just call them out and I will write them down. We're interested in a quantity of good ideas, not determining their merit as yet."

   Note: If there is hesitation, the Leader might begin with deciding (1) when to wake up, (2) what to wear, (3) what to eat, (4) when to leave for work, (5) getting the kids off to school, etc. The Leader might encourage participants to really "get into" the brainstorm by getting into it him/herself. Activities and decisions can be written inside the square, or beside it with an arrow to the appropriate space. Also the Leader should try to avoid getting mired in details of the entire day — a sample will do. The Leader might also gently encourage each person to participate.

2. "Now the inner square represents all activities you can do and decisions you can make when you are able to move freely about but are sick with a terminal illness. How many of the things that we have up in the outer square can we copy into this inner square, and how many are no longer possible or plausible for whatever reason?"
   Note: The Leader might take time to encourage participants to verbalize why some activities or decisions might not be possible in the second box.

3. "The inner circle represents all activities you can do and all decisions you can make when you are confined to bed with a terminal illness. Now we will have to use our imaginations a little bit because this is not an easy task. Which activities can we copy into the inner circle?"

Debriefing

1. How easy was it for you to image the kinds of activities and decisions a terminally ill person might make?
2. Which activities and decisions would be most difficult for you to give up?
3. How do you imagine you might handle being confined to bed with an illness that was not terminal, such as the flu? How might you handle being confined to bed with a terminal illness? What might you want from your loved ones to assist you in handling this kind of situation?

17. Aging: Wrinkles of Time

Goals

1. To sensitize individuals to the reality of the aging process and the inevitability of old age.
2. To elicit participants' attitudes and feelings about old age.
3. To heighten participants' appreciation of their current level of vitality and mobility.

Materials

Several small mirrors or access to a large mirror (as in a dressing room); talcum powder, several different shades of moist make-up base; cold cream; brown eyebrow pencil — blunt ended; ball of string or twine.

Time   1.5 hours.

Procedures

Instruct participants to work in pairs, selecting a partner with whom they are relatively comfortable. Using the powder, make-up base, and eyebrow pencil each will then take 15 minutes to make up the face and hair of the other to simulate a person of seventy years or more. The most potent effect is obtained by first applying the make-up base over the entire face and neck and then using the eyebrow pencil to outline wrinkles and provide shading. The contours of the individual's own smile and frown wrinkles and the photograph of the face of an elderly person both serve as realistic guides for the make-up process.

The talcum powder is used to highlight shading on the face and neck and to whiten head and facial hair. The emotional impact of viewing oneself upon completion of this process is commensurate with the time and effort the partner devotes to making up the individual. Hence, careful attention to the process is encouraged. The facilitator may serve as a technical advisor to participants throughout the process. When the make-up process has been completed, participants are directed to spend a few minutes viewing themselves in the mirror and paying attention to their reactions. At this time, discussion points 1 through 4 might be addressed, or the facilitator may choose to proceed directly to the next activity and postpone all discussion until the end.

For the second segment of the exercise, participants then are instructed to cut from the roll of twine approximately 3 feet of string. They are then to tie their right and left leg together at the ankles such that there are about 8-12 inches of string between their two feet. Participants then are directed to mill around the room, interacting with one another as if at a social gathering. Approximately 15 minutes should be allowed for the preparation and the milling, after which participants are called together for a discussion of the experience.

Debriefing

Pose the following questions as participants view themselves in a mirror:

1. What was your first reaction upon seeing yourself in the mirror?
2. What sort of thoughts come to mind as you look at yourself at age 70?
3. How do you feel about yourself? About the others?
4. Do you feel more or less valuable? Energetic? Productive? Confident? Involved? Capable?
5. How does it feel to have your mobility impaired?
6. How does it feel to have your freedom limited? Your choices reduced?
7. In what ways does it change the way you think about yourself?
8. With the binding removed, how does it feel to have your agility returned?

Variations and special considerations

1. It is essential that the facilitator have already experienced the process both of being made up and of making up another individual so that they may better anticipate and more effectively debrief participants' reactions to the exercise. It is in fact helpful if the facilitator has him/herself been made up immediately prior to the beginning of this session so that he may (1) serve as a model of the end product and (2) be free to provide technical assistance throughout the process.

2. Depending upon the shared history and the trust level within the group, it might be constructive for the facilitator first to demonstrate the make-up process with a member of the group. This is particularly true if there has been no precedent established for touching among group members. Through matter-of-fact attention to the make-up task, the facilitator can establish an atmosphere in which anxiety about touching and being touched is minimized.

3. It is suggested that as participants view themselves in the mirror and as they interact at the "social gathering", the facilitator direct them to monitor (though not necessarily alter) their laughter and joking. Laughter can be a means of diffusing the anxiety associated with altered appearance and mobility, and can detract from the impact of the experience unless participants are aware of the function it is serving.

4. It is also suggested that non-allergenic make-up be used, and that cold cream be available for removal of make-up upon completion of the exercise.

18. The Alarm Clock

Goals

1. To heighten individual's awareness of the finiteness of the time allotted them.
2. To permit participants to examine their manner of coping with limited time.
3. To permit people to examine their manner of coping with constraints upon their involvement with persons and tasks.
4. To permit an examination of their manner of coping with arbitrary events.

Arbitrary and unexpected termination of participants' activities provides a parallel to the realization that one's death is pending.

Materials

One alarm clock for each participant, masking tape, felt tip pens, extra chairs arranged facing the walls away from the central work area.

Time   Exercise adaptable to time available; minimum of 60 minutes.

Procedures

Each participant is instructed to bring an alarm clock, or if possible, the facilitator may provide a clock for each individual. The facilitator clearly prints the name of each participant on a piece of masking tape and places each piece of tape on the front of a separate clock. Each participant is told to note which clock is theirs. The facilitator then randomly sets each alarm to go off at a different time during the ensuing class or workshop period. (Optimal impact is obtained when alarms on one or two of the clocks actually are not set at all.) Clocks should be placed far enough apart that each participant will know when his alarm has rung, and far enough from the participant that he cannot see the time for which the alarm is set. Participants are instructed that when the alarm on an individual's clock goes off, he must stop immediately participating in what he is doing, move to a chair facing the wall, and remain there until further notification by the facilitator. The facilitator should reconvene the total group 20-30 minutes before the end of the session for purposes of debriefing the experience.

The alarm clock exercise is most effective when superimposed upon other activities which require maximal participant involvement. For instance, it might best be employed in conjunction with another structured experience, an active group discussion, or a planning task in which all individuals are engaged. It would be least effective when undertaken during a presentation by the facilitator or any one member of the group.

Debriefing

Discussion of this experience can include exploration of participants' reactions to the following:

a. The interruption,
b. its arbitrariness,
c. its unexpectedness,
d. being excluded from the task,
e. being isolated from other participants,
f. being left behind as others are forced to leave the task,
g. the control exercised by the facilitator,
h. the realization that some participants' alarms never sounded.

Participants can be asked how the awareness that they might have to disengage affected their involvement in the task. They might then be asked how they would have behaved differently had they known *when* they would be forced to stop.

Expressions of frustration, helplessness, anger, (often directed towards the facilitator) and eventual detachment are common in reaction to this exercise. As these feelings are expressed, parallels can be drawn gently to receiving the diagnosis of a terminal illness or the occurrence of an incapacitating injury. This awareness often leads to a degree of resolution on the part of some participants to "live life more fully" while there is the opportunity.

19. Attending Your Own Funeral

Goals

1. To assist individuals in clarifying feelings and values related to funerals and, specifically, their own funerals.
2. To acquaint individuals with the finality of their own deaths.
3. To offer individuals an opportunity to evaluate certain aspects of their lives.

Through guided fantasy, the individual is conducted through the experience of their own funeral. One thereby reviews and evaluates aspects of their life, including the quality of interpersonal relationships.

Materials

A room in which participants can lie comfortably on their backs not touching other participants.

Time   1 to 1.5 hours.

Procedures

Instructions for the guided fantasy are as follows:

"Those of you who wear contact lenses might want to remove them, as I will be asking to have your eyes closed for a while. Now lie on your back, legs uncrossed, and make yourself as comfortable as you can. Close your eyes and just let all the events and worries of the day roll around in your mind. *(Pause)* And when you're ready, leave all those thoughts behind and just appreciate how peaceful and relaxed you feel. Pay attention to those places where you feel tense, and let those parts of your body relax. *(Pause)* Take a deep breath, hold it and let it out slowly.

You are in complete control of your own imagination now, so just follow along with what I am saying as long as you are willing.

[From this point on, the fantasy is adapted from one which appears in Laura Huxley's book, *You Are Not the Target* (New York: Farrar, Strauss, Giroux, 1963)].

Now let your body go. Imagine that the life is gone out of it. Do not speak or move.

Imagine that you have died. Your body is passive, lifeless, useless. Your body is discarded. Your funeral is about to take place.

You are now going to your own funeral.

Look at the people who have come to your funeral. What do they feel? *(Pause)* How do they look at your body? Do they need consolation? *(Pause)* Are they happy to be alive? Would they like to be dead? What are their emotions? *(Pause)*

Look at the people coming to say a last goodbye to this discarded body. Look at each of them. Is there one among them to whom you would like to say something, to explain something, to express a certain feeling? *(Pause)* You cannot do it. Without your power of speech, of writing, of moving — without your body you can do nothing.

Look again at the people who attend your funeral. What would you like to say to each of them, if you could speak? *(Pause)* How would you express yourself to this or that person, if you had a body? *(Pause)*

Do you have a problem which has been difficult to solve? Do you have a decision which has been difficult to make? *(Pause)* Your problem, your decision might become clearer at this moment.

Did you look at the flowers people sent you? What kind are they? How many are there? Did the people try to suit the preferences of the person you were? Or did they only do what they thought they ought to do?

Is anyone giving the eulogy? What is he/she saying? *(Pause)* Does it seem to you sensible, reasonably true to you and your life?

Is there music? Has someone chosen it who knew what you liked, what you would prefer?

Now turn your attention to the person whom you disliked ... or who irritated or repelled you more than any other in your life. *(Pause)* Is there anything you want to say to that person? *(Pause)*

Say it *(in your imagination).*

And now look at the one or ones you love the most, at the one or ones to whom you are most grateful. *(Pause) (In your imagination)* say whatever you ... feel like saying ...

This is your last party. Speak to everyone there, tell them all about yourself, about your mistakes and your suffering, *(pause),* about your love and your longings *(pause).* No longer do you need to protect yourself, no longer do you need to hide behind a wall or a suit of armor. It is your last party: you can explode, you can be miserable or pitiful, insignificant or despicable. At your funeral you can be yourself. *(Pause)*

And now it is over. Come back to your living body.

Acknowledge it and respect it. Feel the life flowing in it. Feel your heart beat. Notice your breathing.

When you're ready, let your attention come back to this room. Now I'm going to count backwards slowly from 5 to 1. When I reach 1, I want you to open your eyes and you will feel alert and rested. Okay. 5 ... 4 ... 3 ... 2 ... 1. Open your eyes, *(pause)* sit up, and look around you.''

Some individuals are able to fantasize better than others. The instructor should reassure participants that it is alright if they experience difficulty in placing themselves into the fantasy.

In processing the guided fantasy, one must attend to underreaction as well as overreaction on the part of the participants. Not only does fantasy focus the individual inward, but also the content of this fantasy emphasizes the ultimate aloneness of each individual. It becomes all the more important, then, to know the state of mind in which each participant leaves this experience.

Debriefing

Before a fantasy is debriefed, it is wise to communicate to the participants some reassurance and some guidelines for constructive processing of individual fantasies.

1. Your fantasy is strictly yours to keep or to share as you please. Feel no pressure to disclose your fantasy. If you choose to share it with the group, you may do so in part or in full.
2. If your fantasy involves another person, these are *your* imaginings about the relationship between you and that other person. Should you decide to share your fantasy with that person, it might provide a valuable springboard from which to discuss your feelings and thoughts with each other. (This guideline mitigates against individuals' viewing their fantasies as absolute truth rather than as suggestion. It also places emphasis upon

the *interaction* highlighted by the fantasy, as opposed to assigning responsibility, guilt or blame for the fantasy to one party or the other.) After such reassurance is offered the following debriefing questions can be employed.

a. What was the experience like for you?
b. Would you like to share any part of your fantasy?
c. Was there any part of your fantasy that was especially meaningful to you?
d. Did you discover anything about your preferences regarding your own funeral?
e. Did anything about the way you are living your life become clearer to you?
f. Did you experience any realizations about persons in your life? About your relationships in general?
g. Did you discover any unfinished business that you might like to pursue at this time?

20. Bambi Excerpt

Goals

1. To provide a fairly open-ended tale which has several analogies to the aging process, dying, and loss.
2. To reflect on the ways in which the cycle of life is portrayed in other than human terms, with particular appeal to a child's discussion of death with a parent or other adult.

Materials

Excerpt from *Bambi*, reprinted below.

Time   20-30 minutes.

Procedures

This excerpt from a literary classic is best given as a reading without interruption and followed by some soliciting of audience response to the story and its meanings, interpretations, etc. Obviously, a rehearsal or two for sense, inflection, timing and the like are needed beforehand, and it may even be helpful to "stage" the reading a bit by using muted lighting, having participants close their eyes to facilitate picturing the scenario being described.

Briefly, the chapter is a vignette wherein two leaves of advanced age converse about their fates as fall sets in. They review their "lives" and the meaning of their relationship to one another, as well as the effects of aging and concerns over impending "death". It is also worth reading *prior* to telling the audience of its origin, or the title of the book.

The leaves were falling from the great oak at the meadow's edge. They were falling from all the trees.

One branch of the oak reached high above the others and stretched far out over the meadow. Two leaves clung to its very tip.

"It isn't the way it used to be," said one leaf to the other.

"No," the other leaf answered. "So many of us have fallen off tonight we're almost the only ones left on our branch."

"You never know who's going to go next," said the first leaf. "Even when it was warm and the sun shone, a storm or a cloudburst would come sometimes, and many leaves were torn off, though they were still young. You never know who's going to go next."

"The sun seldom shines now," sighed the second leaf, "and when it does it gives no warmth. We must have warmth again."

"Can it be true," said the first leaf, "can it really be true, that others come to take our places when we're gone and after them still others, and more and more?"

"It is really true," whispered the second leaf. "We can't even begin to imagine it, it's beyond our powers."

"It makes me very sad," added the first leaf.

They were silent a while. Then the first leaf said quietly to herself, "Why must we fall? ..."

The second leaf asked, "What happens to us when we have fallen?"

"We sink down ..."

"What is under us?"

From: Salten, F., *Bambi*. N.Y.: Simon & Schuster, 1929 (Chapter 8 — all, pp. 72-75).

The first leaf answered, "I don't know, some say one thing, some another, but nobody knows."

The second leaf asked, "Do we feel anything, do we know anything about ourselves when we're down there?"

The first leaf answered, "Who knows? Not one of all those down there has ever come back to tell us about it."

They were silent again. Then the first leaf said tenderly to the other, "Don't worry so much about it, you're trembling."

"That's nothing," the second leaf answered, "I tremble at the least thing now. I don't feel so sure of my hold as I used to."

"Let's not talk any more about such things," said the first leaf.

The other replied, "No, we'll let be. But — what else shall we talk about?" She was silent, but went on after a little while, "Which of us will go first?"

"There's still plenty of time to worry about that," the other leaf assured her, "Let's remember how beautiful it was, how wonderful, when the sun came out and shone so warmly that we thought we'd burst with life. Do you remember? And the morning dew, and the mild and splendid nights . . ."

"Now the nights are dreadful," the second leaf complained, "and there is no end to them."

"We shouldn't complain," said the first leaf gently. "We've outlived many, many others."

"Have I changed much?" asked the second leaf shyly but determinedly.

"Not in the least," the first leaf assured her. "You only think so because I've got to be so yellow and ugly. But it's different in your case."

"You're fooling me," the second leaf said.

"No, really," the first leaf exclaimed eagerly, "believe me, you're as lovely as the day you were born. Here and there may be a little yellow spot but it's hardly noticeable and only makes you handsomer, believe me."

"Thanks," whispered the second leaf, quite touched. "I don't believe you, not altogether; but I thank you because you're so kind, you've always been so kind to me. I'm just beginning to understand how kind you are."

"Hush," said the other leaf, and kept silent herself for she was too troubled to talk any more.

Then they were both silent. Hours passed. A moist wind blew, cold and hostile, through the tree-tops. "Ah, now," said the second leaf, "I . . ." Then her voice broke off. She was torn from her place and spun down. Winter had come.

Debriefing

1. Did you like it?
2. What did you like? Not like?
3. What were the leaves "conversing" about? Why were they talking about it? How did they feel?
4. Have you ever heard anyone else talk like that? Have you ever talked with anyone else like that? If so, how did you feel at the time?
5. How did you feel when the leaf fell?
6. Do you recognize the passage? (give answer)
7. Can you see using this in anyway to help introduce death as a fact of life to a child?

21. Burying Part of the Past

Goals

1. To assist participants in identifying:
   a. thoughts
   b. feelings
   c. values
   d. goals
   e. assumptions once held in the past but since "dispatched".
2. To provide a framework wherein participants might recognize that the development of new dimensions of self involves the discarding of old viewpoints.
3. To promote exploration and discussion regarding the natural occurrence of change, loss, and separation as being an inherent part of the developmental aging process.

An important aspect of the aging person's development is moving beyond old beliefs and attitudes that once influenced how we viewed ourselves and the world around us. Should we fail to do so by clinging to "youthful" visions of ourselves, the development of valuable new dimensions of experience can be impeded. This exercise is designed to assist participants in identifying some of the beliefs, values, goals and assumptions that were important at an earlier age, but since have changed in importance. By going through a ritual of "burying" past images of themselves, participants are assisted in exploring ways loss and separation are a natural part of the aging process and how loss sets the stage for continued creative discovery.

Materials

Each participant is asked to bring a picture of themselves taken several years in the past. If pictures are not available, the Leader could provide paper and pen to each participant and ask each to draw a rough sketch of how they looked several years ago.

Time   Approximately one hour.

Procedures

1. The Leader asks that each participant have available a picture of themselves taken several years ago. If pictures are not available, each participant is asked to draw a picture of themselves, as if the picture was a "snapshot" from the past.
2. Then s/he asks each person to take a close look at their own picture and try to remember vividly what their life experience was like then.
3. Each participant is then asked to write their responses to the following:
   a. When I was that age, 3 things I was excited about were:
   b. When I was that age, 3 things I was afraid of were:
   c. When I was that age, 3 things I felt proud of were:
   d. When I was that age, 3 goals I had were:
4. Then, the facilitator asks each participant to go back over their responses and to check those that no longer "fit" for the participant. Next, they write their checked responses on the back of their pictures.
5. The Leader next asks all the participants to form a close circle. Each person, in turn, is invited to place his picture face down in the center of the circle. As he does so, the participant is invited to say "goodbye" to the parts from his/her past that no longer fit, to "bury" them.
6. After participants have placed their pictures in the circle, they are all asked to close their eyes and reflect on the various meanings this experience may have had for them.

7. After debriefing, those who wish to may retrieve their picture for personal "disposition."

Debriefing

Some of the following questions may help to promote discussion:

1. What was this experience like for you?
2. What parts from your past still fit for you?
3. What was it like for you to say goodbye to feelings and thoughts from the past?
4. What current beliefs, goals, values do you imagine might change in the coming years? Which are likely to remain the same?

22. The Clothes We Wear

Goals

1. To assist individuals in identifying important personal values they live by.
2. To assist individuals in exploring their feelings about dying.

The values that we live by are often reflected in the clothing we wear. In this exercise, participants are asked to select three pieces of clothing they would choose to wear at their own funerals. Through this exercise, participants are given the opportunity to identify the values these clothing articles signify to them personally. By asking the participants to select three articles of clothing, they are given the chance to prioritize these values as well as identify them.

Materials   Paper and pencil for each participant.

Time   Approximately 45-60 minutes.

Procedures

1. The Leader asks each participant to imagine that they each have only one week left to live.
2. The participants are then asked to imagine the following: "During the coming week you go to your clothes closet and carefully select what you will wear at your own funeral. You pick three different articles of clothing that mean a great deal to you. Each piece of clothing seems to say a lot about you and the way you tried to live. What three pieces do you choose?"
3. Participants are then asked to write down the articles of clothing and briefly describe the meaning attached to each.
4. The instructor may decide to divide the participants into small groups for discussion.

Debriefing

1. What articles of clothing did you select?
2. How did you go about making the decision?
3. What are some of the values reflected by your clothing choice?
4. How much time do you currently spend wearing the kind of clothing you chose? Enough or not?
5. What articles of clothing might your loved ones select for you? Your parents? Your mate? Your best friend? Are these clothing selections made by your loved ones for you similar to your own selections? What might this say about how well they currently know you?

23. Communication in the Face of Impending Loss

Goals:

1. To raise the individual's awareness of ways that s/he might relate to dying persons.
2. To suggest alternate hypotheses for the behavior of aged and dying persons.
3. To sensitize the individual to some aspects of the experience of dying and aging persons.
4. To highlight the effects of non-attention upon communication and thought processes.
5. To teach the value of listening.

This exercise provides an analog to the progressive isolation of the dying individual. Behaviors commonly labeled as senility in the aged and withdrawal in the dying are reinterpreted as natural responses to discomfort and ineffective listening on the part of others.

Materials   A watch or clock with a second hand.

Time   30-45 minutes.

Procedures

Groups of 4 or 5 are formed. One group member takes responsibility for keeping the time limits. Each person takes 2 minutes in which to talk about something that is important to him/her. The other group members are instructed not to attend to the person who is speaking at the time. They are to avoid eye contact with the speaker and to give *no* verbal or non-verbal response. The speaker is to talk for the full two minutes, after which the role of speaker will rotate to the next individual. Any discussion of reactions should be postponed until each person has taken the role of speaker.

Variations

It may be desirable to give the "avoid attending" instructions to the group while the "speaker" is outside the room. The speaker could be asked to think about some personally significant issue to present to the group.

Debriefing

1. What was the experience like for you?
2. What were you experiencing as the speaker?
3. What were you feeling toward the members of your group?
4. What were you experiencing as the "non-listener"?
5. What were you feeling toward the Leaders? About the instructions?
6. As the speaker, what did you find yourself doing? Rambling? Forgetting? Repeating yourself? Clamming up?
7. What were you not getting from your group members that you wanted?
8. What kept you from trying harder to get it?
9. How did you feel about yourself when you finished speaking?

Debriefing may then lead to discussion of (1) the participants' responses to their own grandparents, parents or other aging and dying individuals, (2) our own roles in isolating aging and dying individuals and/or (3) disengagement theory, senility, and societal and institutional views of aging and dying.

24. Draw a Feeling: "I'm Living" and "I'm D[

Goals

1. To enable individuals to reflect on their particular associat[
   life and living.
2. To provide a minimal structure for facilitating discussion.

Through the use of a drawing activity, this exercise makes possible the [
perceptual dimensions which might not be revealed in a more formal method. Because o[
the ambiguous nature of the drawings, participants are able to express and explore their
feelings about dying and living both from the activity of drawing and from interpreting the
drawings of others.

Materials

Two sheets of paper for each participant; crayons or pencils.
The title for each sheet is:

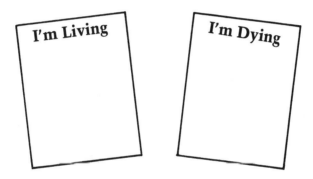

Time   50 minutes.

Procedures

1. Instruct participants to sit in a circle. In large groups (over 15), two circles could be
   formed.
2. Give each participant a sheet of blank paper with title "I'm Dying" written at the top.
   The Leader gives the following instructions: "Take a few moments and reflect. Then
   draw a picture that shows what you would feel if you fully knew you were dying soon.
   The picture you draw does not have to be highly artistic or realistic, only an expression
   of what you feel." The Leader might allow 10-15 minutes for each person to complete
   his/her picture.
3. The Leader then gives each participant another sheet of paper with the title "I'm Living". "Take a few moments again and reflect. Then draw a picture that shows what you
   feel when you fully know you are living." Allow 10-15 minutes for each person to
   complete drawing.
4. Alternate methods of group discussion:
   a. Ask each person in turn to share their drawings of "I'm Dying" and "I'm Living"
      with the rest of the group, describing what is portrayed in their own drawings.
   b. Ask participants to shuffle and redistribute the drawings to others in the group. Each
      person then describes what she/he sees in the drawing she/he now holds. An advan-
      tage of this method is that it allows the artist to remain anonymous.

...e three basic variations used to date with this SLE. First, as each person describes ...s/he sees in the pictures, the Leader could make a master list of all that has been ...ciated with each term, "I'm Living" and "I'm Dying", to use as a stimulus for discus-...on. Or, the pictures could be replaced verbally thus: Ask each participant to take out a blank sheet of paper and write the words "Death is . . ." at the top of one side. Then they are instructed to complete the phrase with as many thoughts as come to mind in 5 minutes keeping to the one side of the page.

Once that is done, the Leader then tells the group to turn their papers over and write the root words "Life is . . ." and take 5 more minutes to complete as many thoughts as will fill that side of the page.

Debriefing this variation can be done in several configurations from pairs to small groups, focusing on comparisons and contrasts in the responses each wrote, as well as looking at similarities and differences between each side of one's paper. The objective again here is to allow the sentence completion format to enable some freer, open-ended production of de-scriptions to emerge for discussion and recognition purposes. The frequent use of metaphor and simile should correspond to the feelings of difficulty often expressed when one tries to "define" death. Often, the major ways of doing so are in terms which negate some living process, or which view them as stark opposites. This variation can be done fruitfully in about 30 minutes.

Still another variation on the incomplete sentence idea is that suggested by Joan McNeil of Kansas State. In asking participants to write responses to "Death is . . ." and later "Life is . . ." she sometimes has them limit their completion to a single sentence. Then they are collected and arranged in some fairly cohesive order to produce a "class/group poem" which is then copied and distributed. This often produces some unique compositions, and gives all the participants a sense of contribution. The product can then be used as the topic for small group discussion, with similar lines of inquiry as noted above.

25. Eulogy

Goals

1. To invite individuals to confront the inevitability that their lives will end.
2. To provide people with a perspective from which to view the whole of their lives.
3. To permit individuals to preview the feelings they might experience about themselves in looking back on their lives.
4. To offer people an opportunity to examine any discrepancies between their values/goals/priorities and the way they currently conduct their lives. By means of constructing the "story" of one's life and hearing that story read by another individual, the participant is able to obtain a broader perspective upon self, the past, present, and future.

Materials   Paper and pencils.

Time   Twenty-five minutes and five additional minutes *per* participant.

Procedures   Instruct participants as follows:

Your task is to write the eulogy that you wish it were possible and realistic to have delivered about you at your funeral. A eulogy is to be distinguished from an obituary which appears in the newspaper as notification of your death. Don't write the eulogy that could be delivered if you died tomorrow, unless that represents all you want to be in the future. So give yourself time, hope, and even allow yourself some fantasy and wishful thinking, in constructing your story. This exercise requires reflection, silence, being alone with yourself, so take the next 20 minutes to compose a eulogy to your life.

When participants have completed their eulogies, direct them to look around the group and find someone (a) with whom they feel comfortable, or (b) whom they like and trust or (c) who is important to them. (Facilitator should select the phrase which most appropriately fits the group's level of trust and cohesiveness.)

Instruct participants to give their eulogies to that person to be read aloud to the group. Those who receive eulogies of other participants should look over them and be sure they can read them clearly. Then each eulogy should be read aloud carefully, as if the reader were actually responsible to the person for communicating the essence of his or her life.

Variation

Rather than writing a euology participants may wish to construct a collage or other visual eulogy. Magazines, scissors, tacking paper, glue and other art materials would be necessary for this variation. Participants would need to explain their art work to the partner for presentation.

Debriefing

1. What was that experience like for you?
2. What was it like to write your eulogy? What did you find easy or difficult? Why?
3. Did you discover anything about yourself or your life?
4. What was it like to read someone else's eulogy?
5. How was it to hear your own eulogy read? What feelings did this evoke? What thoughts did it trigger?
6. In the process of writing and hearing your eulogy, did you discover any discrepancies between your goals or dreams and the way you live your life now? Do you want to reduce these discrepancies? How might you do this in the immediate future?

26. Giving It All Away

Goals

1. To assist participants in exploring and identifying feelings associated with an aspect of the dying process: giving up our prized possessions to people we love.
2. To provide a structure wherein participants can freely explore and discuss feelings of attachment and loss.

In our culture, few of us take the time to write our "wills" until we have reason to believe that our death is imminent. The assumption is commonly made that a will is not necessary until our elder years. Even then "wills" are often written in a language that does not adequately convey the personal feelings and meaning involved. This exercise is designed to assist participants in exploring the feelings that might be associated with this process of giving up our prized possessions and leaving them to the persons of our own choosing.

Materials

Paper and pencil for each participant — 10 sheets per person. A small grill or heat resistant container in which to burn the paper.

Time Approximately 1.5-2 hours.

Procedures

1. The Leader might begin this exercise by briefly restating the rationale. S/he then would instruct each person to find a comfortable area in the room where s/he might each work alone. The Leader gives each participant a pencil and ten sheets of paper.
2. The Leader instructs participants to think about 10 prized possessions they each currently own. S/he asks that each write the name of each possession on a separate sheet of paper. After each possession, they are asked to briefly write what they value most about the possession. Then, for each possession, the participants are asked to choose some person they would most like to give that possession to. The participants are asked to choose a different person for each possession.
3. The Leader then asks the participants to form a close circle. Each participant, in turn, is then asked to describe one of their possessions, what value it holds for them, who they would give it to, and why. After a participant has described one possession, he folds the sheet of paper and places it in the center of the circle. The turn is then passed to another participant. The same procedure is followed, until one-by-one, all 10 possessions have been described by each person and placed in the center of the circle.
4. The Leader then asks participants to watch silently as s/he places all the paper in a grill and sets them to flame.
5. The Leader might encourage participants to sit silently and reflect a few minutes on the meaning this experience has had for them.

Debriefing

The Leader might facilitate group discussion by asking some of the following questions:

1. What was this experience like for you?
2. What kind of feelings did you become aware of during this experience?
3. What was it like for you to describe your valued possessions?
4. What was it like to try to choose some person to give your possessions to?
5. What kind of feelings do you now have about your possessions? Your loved ones?
6. What feelings do you now have about writing "wills"?

27. Living Wages

Goals

1. To assist each participant in examining their "everyday" lifestyle to determine how fulfilling that lifestyle is for him/her.
2. To allow each participant to compare how they view their own lifestyle with the group's evaluation of his/her lifestyle.
3. To assist participants in developing the ability to evaluate their own lifestyles in order to make satisfying changes where appropriate.
4. To give participants opportunity to identify specific ways they might improve the quality of their everyday living.

We can often go through an entire day, hustling and bustling, without pausing to reflect on how satisfied we are with the style and quality of our lives that day. Pausing to reflect gives us an opportunity to re-evaluate and make appropriate adjustments. Adjustments can then be made that are geared to give us a more complete sense of personal fulfillment in our everyday activities. This exercise is designed to assist participants in taking a close look at their everyday style of living and the value they place on their own particular lifestyle.

Materials

1. Blank checks
2. Envelopes
3. Pencils or pens

Time   Approximately one hour.

Procedures

1. The facilitator explains to the group that each participant will have an opportunity to evaluate how satisfied they are with the way they have conducted their life that day. The Leader asks each participant, in turn, to come to the middle of the room and write themself a check. Explain that the pay scale ranges from $0.00 to $1,000.00. If the participant feels s/he has lived fully and completely that day, s/he should pay themself a large amount. If the participant feels dissatisfied about the way they have lived that day, s/he should pay themself a small amount.

2. As each person completes writing themself a check, s/he is instructed to put their "paycheck" in an envelope, write their name on the outside, and then seal the envelope. All the envelopes are then collected by the Leader.

3. At random, select an envelope and ask the selected participant to take a seat in the middle of the circle. The participant is requested to open their own envelope and reveal to the group the amount paid himself or herself and why. At this point, the group members might be invited to give their impressions to the participant about the following: Is the individual's pay similar to what other group members would pay? If not, what are some of the differences between the way the individual views and values his/her style of living and the way other group members view it? (**Note:** The Leader might prepare the group by providing guidelines for giving constructive feedback.).

4. When all participants have revealed their checks in the middle of the circle and received feedback, the Leader facilitates a discussion of the experience.

Variation

The Leader might request each participant to imagine they each would die during the coming week. Each participant is then instructed to write themself a check that would reflect how satisfied they had been with the quality of their entire life thus far.

Debriefing

1. How easy/difficult was it for you today to place a dollar value on yourself and the way you live? On your fellow group members and the way they live?
2. What may account for some of the differences between the way you view your life style now and the way the group viewed it?
3. If you had evaluated yourself and given yourself a "paycheck" one year ago, what would you have given then? Why?
4. What are some specific things you might do in the immediate future to increase the "worth" or quality of your living?

28. Loss As Opportunity for Growth*

Goals

1. To help death educators and others in the helping professions give individuals who have experienced losses another perspective on loss.
2. To depict loss experience as part of a process, continuum and framework which can lead to personal growth.
3. To utilize nonverbal methods for fantasy exploration, paving the way for creativity and reintegration.

Materials Pastels or soft crayons, large sheets of paper for each participant.

Time 2 to 3 hours.

Procedures

Participants are requested to select a partner who, if possible, they do not know. For ten minutes they exchange names, briefly relate their particular loss and share something positive related to the present or the future. Examples: something good to eat, a rewarding activity, someone they love, etc.

Pairs are then asked to join together with another dyad to become groups of four. Each member of the original dyad introduces their partner to the others in their small group. The four interact among themselves relating their current experience focusing on feelings, insights, physical sensations and whatever else they wish. Drawing paper and drawing materials are now distributed.

Directions: "You are asked to draw three pictures. Draw in any way you choose. Skill is irrelevant. You will have approximately 15 minutes for each expression (picture). The first drawing is about you and your world before your loss."

When they have finished, "Now draw you and your world in the present."

Finally, "A possible future. If there is any bright place, try and include anyone or anything you feel will help you reach that place. If for now there is no bright place see if there is anyone or anything that can help you in your darkness and incorporate that person or thing."

Next, ask participants to share their pictures with their original group of four. After about fifteen minutes, ask them to select one they are willing to share with the whole group. Within the context of a supportive environment, group discussion should follow.

Debriefing

1. How did you feel as you drew each picture?
2. Did you learn anything about yourself as you were drawing?
3. In what ways are the pictures alike?
4. What do you see as the role of the future from your picture?
5. Did others see things in your pictures which you were not aware of?
6. Was it difficult to show your pictures to others?
7. Were your pictures in any way similar to those of others?
8. How did you feel about seeing others' pictures?
9. How did the first part of the exercise relate to the rest?
10. Do you see your loss on a continuum? Do you view others' pictures and loss as part of a continuum?

---

*Suggested by Dorree Waldbaum, Annapolis, MD.

29. Me and My Name: A Past and Future Projected Fantasy.

Goals

1. To assist participants in developing an increased awareness of the inevitability of death.
2. To provide participants with an opportunity to review, in fantasy, some of the stages of development they have accomplished and some future stages of development they will eventually experience.

Our names are intimately linked with our own personal conception of who we are. By focusing on this one aspect of identity, this exercise gently leads participants into reviewing their life chronology, imagining future events and the inevitability of death.

Setting   Space enough so that participants can stretch out.

Time   Approximately one hour.

Procedures

1. Instruct participants to find a comfortable area where they can stretch out, relax, and become aware of themselves.
2. One may then give brief suggestions for enhancing relaxation and increasing self awareness: breathing deeply, closing eyes, focusing on body temperature, etc.
3. The Leader then begins a slow-paced structured fantasy during which s/he describes cues for recollections, past memories, and future projections. The Leader slowly gives concrete, vivid memory cues focusing on one particular aspect of the participant's past and future experiences — the participant's name.

It might be good to elaborate on the following examples:

a. The memory of seeing one's name written on a birthday cake, noticing the colors and flavor of the cake. Remembering hearing your name being sung in the "Happy Birthday" song.
b. Seeing in your mind's eye a time when you first printed your name with a crayon or pencil.
c. Remembering seeing your name on a report card, noticing the lettering, seeing the grades given. Hearing your teacher call your name.
d. Seeing in your mind's eye your name written on the collar of a shirt or on gym shorts for identification. Remembering the sound of your name being called by your mother.
e. Seeing your name written on a holiday package, noticing the colors and shapes.
f. Remembering hearing your name called to step forward to receive your (high) school diploma; seeing your name written on it.
g. Seeing in your mind's eye your name addressed on the envelope of a love letter. Hearing the sound of your loved one call your name.
h. Imagining seeing in your mind's eye your name written on the cover of Newsweek; on a movie marquee; written in the sky with sky writing. Imagining hearing your name repeated on national TV.
i. Imagining seeing your name written on an admittance form to a hospital. Hearing the physician pronounce your name.
j. Seeing in your mind's eye your name written on your will.
k. Seeing in your mind's eye your name printed on a death certificate. Hearing your loved ones utter your name as they realize you have died.

l. Seeing your name printed in the obituary column of the newspaper.
m. Seeing your name engraved on a tombstone.
n. Imagining your tombstone five years after your death; 100 years after, 1,000 years after.

After allowing several minutes of quiet time, the Leader could terminate the fantasy by asking participants to slowly open their eyes, stretch, sit up, etc. Processing the experience might then occur in small groups or together as a whole group.

Debriefing

1. What was this experience like for you?
2. Which scenes were you most vividly able to visualize in your mind's eye? Which scenes were harder to visualize?
3. What kind of feelings did you experience in response to seeing your name written in these scenes? In response to hearing your name called in the different scenes?
4. What kind of thoughts did this experience stir up for you about the inevitability of dying?

Reference

For possible supplemental reading, cf. Kastenbaum, R., *Death, Society, and Human Experience.* St. Louis: Mosby, 1981 (See esp. chap. 1-4).

30. My Body — Now and Then

Goals

1. To stimulate thought and exploration about a significant change that occurs through the aging process as people approach death: namely, the change in our body strength, resilience, and form.
2. To assist individuals in identifying significant aspects of their body image and exploring their feelings and attitudes about "growing older" in their bodies.

Discussing death and dying necessarily involves discussing the countless variety of losses that death signifies. Obviously, important losses occur in our bodies due to the aging process and ultimately the loss of the body itself through death. This exercise is specifically designed to stimulate thinking about some of those changes/losses associated with our bodies as we approach our own deaths.

Materials Paper and pencils for each participant.

Time Approximately 45 minutes.

Procedures

1. Facilitator presents a brief rationale for the exercise; as above.
2. Each participant is then instructed to draw three pictures of their body.
    Picture number one: Participants are asked to draw a picture of how they look today. In the picture, they are asked to emphasize or exaggerate the area of their body they are most proud of.
    Picture number two: Participants are asked to draw a picture of how they imagine they will look when they are 60 years old. In the picture, they are again asked to give special attention to that body area they are most proud of currently.
    Picture number three: Participants are asked to draw a picture of how they imagine they will look when they are 90 years old and to give special attention to the body area they are most proud of.

Variations

Use of this option depends on the maturity level of the participants and the trust level the group has formed over time. Participants can be asked to draw a picture of their bodies at the moment of death. They are also asked to give special attention to the body part they currently are most proud of.

Debriefing

1. What kind of changes occurred to the body part you were most proud of? How did you feel about these changes?
2. Did other parts of your body change in importance as you grew older? Did some parts become more important?
3. As your body becomes older, what might be some changes in your style of living?
4. Now that you completed this exercise, how do you feel about your bodies now?
5. What are the differences between aging and dying? Should they be equated?

Optional discussion questions if the variation above has been utilized:

6. What was it like for you to imagine your body at the moment of death? What kind of feelings did this stir up?
7. Were you able to complete the picture? If so, what were you thinking as you completed it? If not, what prevented you?

31. The Pecking Order of Death

Goals

1. To provide a "guided fantasy" experience in anticipating loss.
2. To assist participants to take stock of the "significant others" in their life space.
3. To enable people to gain a perspective on the meanings of death occurring both in and out of turn/season.

This is an exercise in self-exploration designed to give participants a different view of who they value and how they prize those relationships in light of their death-loss. It can assist the learner in defining anew the importance placed on renewal and recognition of those living persons and the potential effects of their death — as well as one's own — in time.

Setting

Preferably a closed room where light can be dimmed or shut out; one free from other distracting noise, intrusions, etc. and one having comfortable seats.

Time   Approximately 30-40 minutes (expandable).

Procedures

Introduce the coming experience as a guided fantasy, a brief experiment in exploring one's so-called "place" in life (in death). Indicate that it will help to dim the lights, have their eyes gently closed, and get comfortable in their seats. Then, direct them through the following series of thoughts. (It is best to rehearse this with an audio tape or other person before doing it with a large group, particularly so timing and pauses and inflection can be mastered to elicit a satisfactory "imagery" experience.)

"Relax for a moment. When your mind is quiet and without pressure, let a neutral visual field form itself in your mind's eye. When this background field has established itself, visualize the face of somebody you care about, a person who is important to you. See this person's face as though it were a suddenly illuminated light bulb glowing against the non-descript background. Keep this face in view. But now think of somebody else you care about. Watch how this face appears and lights up in your mind's eye as well. You now have the inner presence of two people who are important to you. Now visualize a third person you care about, in the same way as you have visualized the others, who are still present . . . Now a fourth person . . . A fifth person . . . A sixth person . . . A seventh person. Alright, that will do. Your mind now contains visually, explicitly the symbols of seven important people."

"One of these people will die before the others. You do not know for sure who this will be, but you do have a guess or feeling about it. Extinguish that person's face. The light goes out where that face had been; the other lights are still on. Time goes by. Another person dies. Watch this person's light go out. The other lights are on, but now there are two dark spots. More time elapses. Another person dies; another light goes out. Three people gone; four remaining. Which light will be the next to be extinguished? Time goes by, and a fourth light goes out. Only three of your important people remain illuminated in your mind's eye. Now another dies. Which of the remaining two will be the next to die, which the survivor? More time elapses. And another light goes out. Your mind's eye, only a few moments ago populated by some of the people closest and most significant to you, now is dark except for a single face."

"Halt the thought experiment here, but keep your eyes closed and reflect, if you will, upon the following questions:

The survivor in your mind's eye — is this perhaps the youngest of the important people you visualized at the outset?

The first person to die — was it perhaps the oldest of the important people you visualized at the outset?

As individuals continued to die, did you continue to respond implicitly to each death in its full particularity — or, at a certain point, did the mass of accumulated loss take precedence over specific bereavement?

In what ways did your thoughts and feelings fluctuate between concern for those who were gone and those who were remaining? Did you find your mind and your heart divided between the living and the dead?

One final question, if you will: Where does your own face, your own life and fate, belong in this sequence? Would you have been the first to perish? The last? Who of these people do you implicitly expect to survive? Who will survive you?"

"Now I'm going to raise the lights again, and ask you to open your eyes slowly and return your thoughts to here and now, where we'll see what kinds of experiences our little thought experiment provided."

Debriefing

Either in small subgroups or with the entire group, some further inquiry along the following lines is needed to gain some reflected closure on the experience.

1. What was the experience like for you? How are you feeling about it now?
2. What were your answers to the questions posed regarding
   — youngest to die
   — oldest to die
   — your probable "place" in the sequence
3. Did the "most important" or "closest" one predecease you or would you die first? What are the implications of that for you? for them?
4. Did you feel "resistant" or unable to envision anyone who came to mind? Why was that? Did it feel real at all?
5. Does this type of experience concern you as "tampering with fate" or "magical thinking" in any way?
6. At some point, did you notice yourself feeling "numbed" at the accumulated loss you sensed.
7. Does this experience say anything to you about your own sense of cherishing your relationships with these people and how you demonstrate that or renew its vitality?

References

Robert Kastenbaum in Datan, N. and Ginsberg, L. (Eds.). *Life-Span Developmental Psychology: Normative Crises and Interventions*. New York: Academic Press, 1976.

32. Planning the Last Day

Goals

1. To heighten awareness of the inevitability of death and sensitivity to issues relating to "interpersonal loss".
2. To promote discussion and insight relating to interpersonal attachments, change, loss, and grief.

All too often, most of us take for granted the people we care most about. With our busy schedules, it can be easy to create the illusion that we have plenty of time to spend with the people we love — tomorrow or the next day. This exercise is designed to promote discussion about the finiteness of life and to assist participants in developing an increased awareness about the quality of their interpersonal living.

Materials   Paper and pencils for participants.

Time   Approximately 1 hour.

Procedure

1. The Leader distributes paper and pencils to each participant. S/he instructs the participants to each find a place in the room where they can reflect comfortably alone.
2. After each participant has secured a comfortable position, the Leader gives the following general instructions.

"Close your eyes and take a few minutes to deeply relax ... (the Leader may want to offer relaxation suggestions here). Now think of some person you know very well and care very much for ... *(pause).* When you have thought of such a person, please indicate by raising your index finger.

After each participant has raised an index finger the Leader continues:

"Imagine that this person will soon have to leave you forever. Before she or he goes, that person asks you to plan an entire day especially for them. They ask you to plan the whole day in a way that would make them very happy. You feel very special that you have such a chance and you begin to plan that day. Think about how you would plan the day and then open your eyes and write down your answers to the following questions.

1. On the day, what time would you arrange for your "special person" to wake up? How would you wake that person up? *(pause)*
2. What would your "special person" like for breakfast? Where would they want to eat it? *(pause)*
3. What clothes would you pick for your "special person" to wear? *(pause)*
4. What would you arrange to do in the morning? *(pause)*
5. What would your "special person" like for lunch? Where? *(pause)*
6. What kind of activities would you plan for the afternoon? With whom? *(pause)*
7. What would your "special person" like for dinner? Where? *(pause)*
8. What would you plan for evening activities? *(pause)*
9. How would you say good-bye at the end of your time together?

(*Note to the Leader:* Because of the emotional intensity of the last question, you might want to talk about the OKness of experiencing feelings).

After an appropriate pause for reflection, the Leader might utilize any of the following discussion strategies.

1. Request that participants form dyads, triads, or small groups to discuss the days they planned and process the experience.
2. Discuss the exercises with the entire group.

Debriefing

1. What was this experience like for you?
2. What was it like for you to try to design a day for someone you care about? What kind of activities did you plan?
3. What feelings did you have about spending the "last" day with your "special person"?
4. How did these feelings affect the way you planned the day? How might these feelings affect the way you might actually spend that last day?
5. How does this exercise and discussion leave you feeling about your "special person"?

33. Renal Dialysis: What's of Worth?

Goals

1. To provide a simulation of what a life-and-death decision might be like with only scarce resources available; one which parallels the everyday bioethical quandaries which characterize modern medical practice.
2. To enable participants to clarify what they value about their lives.
3. To experience problem-solving when few absolutes prevail.
4. To examine what alterations in lifestyle a life-threatening illness can pose.

Setting   Room to accommodate circular seating for each member in a group.

Time   Fifty minutes minimum.

Procedures

1. If not already accomplished, one should precede the exercise with brief self-introductions by all group members.

2. Form the group into a circle where each member may be visible when talking to one another.

3. The experience can be introduced by title and by sharing the goals. Then, the "task" is described thus. "You are a group of outpatients who similarly are suffering from renal failure, i.e. your kidneys are not functioning adequately for your body to eliminate liquid wastes. There are only limited apparatus available locally with which to mechanically supplement the kidney function, and thus you cannot all be offered this lifesaving option. Those of you who cannot find either a satisfactory transplant kidney or secure renal dialysis (the process involving the machine) are facing a shortened life, as those un_eliminated_ wastes will accumulate and poison you fatally in a short time. There are only openings for two persons available at present, and you are to decide which two of you will be given the access to dialysis and who shall be given what amounts to a death sentence."

4. Share the ground rules for discussion with them. They are:
   a. you have only 20 minutes to decide.
   b. you cannot opt out; no self-sacrifices!
   c. you are to argue for your own inclusion, building a case for yourself using only the actual vital data about your life situation as it actually exists.
   d. you may argue for *or* against the inclusion of other members.

5. Some background regarding renal dialysis should be shared prior to beginning discussion. This could include:
   a. without access to the dialysis machine for about 20 hours each week, the person in renal dialysis will not survive for long (a few months on average with complicated deteriorating of other body systems in interim).
   b. because of the scarcity of dialysis machines and kidney donors, some persons with other pre-existing deteriorating or chronic diseases have been denied treatment (by some hospitals) in favor of other, "healthier" candidates, feeling that dialysis may only be a "temporary expedient" in such circumstances.
   c. generally speaking, persons over 40 years of age seem to do less well with dialysis than younger patients, though they do not (obviously) find it useless.

d. "successful" dialysis has, in past experience, been positively correlated with: (may be shared selectivity).
- being married or otherwise having close family support
- being employed prior to renal failure
- being female
- being under or only moderately overweight
- having successfully coped with other (chronic) maladies in past
- having a flexible outlook and coping style
- having had greater than an 8th grade education
- having an active, sectarian religious practice
- having an active, ongoing hobby
- being conformant to rules and regulations ,

6. Give directions to proceed, indicating that you too will be participating, and that "we" have only 20 minutes to reach a decision. Give a warning at 5 and 2 minutes left, and adhere to the time limit.

7. At the end of 20 minutes, regardless of whether or what decision has been made, tell the group to "shift gears" and spend the next 20 minutes discussing (processing, debriefing, whatever . . .) the previous activity.

8. You can refer to the questions below in any way you choose, but the idea is to cover some of the dynamics that went on, and to highlight the individual behaviors and thoughts while accomplishing the stated purposes for the experience.

9. If time allows, you can solicit further comments and reactions, and finish by summarizing what the goals of the exercise were and what implications the experience can have for our consideration of death-related behaviors.

Variations

A role-play simulation using very similar premises was devised by Gerald M. Phillips of Pennsylvania State University and published in 1974. It is described at length in the publication cited below.

Debriefing

1. What were the critical factors influencing your choice, including medical, psychological, family/social, etc.?
2. Did any novel or compromise solutions get proposed? If so, how were they dealt with?
3. What types of behaviors were evident, both in the course of "arguing" for one's selection, and in the process of arriving at a consensus decision?
4. What values were highlighted and treated as significant factors in the course of the selection process? Why?
5. Note how often (or infrequently) mention of *dying, death,* and the possible *vital* consequences of your selection was made.
6. To what extent were you motivated to *avoid* making a decision, perhaps by choosing someone through some "method of chance" such as tossing a coin, drawing straws, etc.? Discuss the implications of such "decision-making" ploys.
7. To what extent did the group attempt to "objectify" an essentially subjective judgment by working out of "formula," point systems, and the like, for rating candidates in some hierarchical manner? Was this effective? Why?
8. Discuss the overall impact of participating in such a decision-making process, particularly as a *real* task.
9. What particular reactions, insights, etc., have you gained from participating in a task, albeit simulated, wherein your personal values, goals, and interpersonal skills were so critical and in focus?

References

The simulated role-play mentioned above as a variant of this SLE can be found in Pfeiffer, J. and Jones, J. (Eds.). *The 1974 Annual Handbook for Group Facilitators.* La Jolla, CA: University Associates, 1974, pp. 78-86.

Also, a useful book providing extensive background on renal dialysis and its psychosocial effects is Czaczkes, J. W. and Kaplan-DeNour, A. *Chronic Hemodialysis as a Way of Life.* New York: Brunner-Mazel, 1978.

34. Rocking Chair Fantasy

Goals

1. To assist individuals in identifying attitudes about their personal past experiences which may be influencing their current feelings about death and dying.

2. To assist individuals in briefly reviewing their lives in order to determine how satisfied they are with their quality and style of living. This exercise may be used as a stimulus for life planning activities.

Acknowledging the inevitability of our own deaths can give us impetus to review the way we have led our lives thus far. Being able to approach an acceptance of the inevitability of our own deaths can also be affected by how satisfied we are with the quality of the life we have led. This exercise is designed to assist individuals in briefly reviewing their lives. Through a guided fantasy experience, participants will be given the opportunity to examine three different "spontaneous memories" from their past. Through individual exploration and group discussion participants may then be assisted in identifying first, life style themes common to each memory and second, ways these life style themes may be currently affecting their attitudes toward dying.

Materials Paper and pencils; a quiet, comfortable environment.

Time Approximately 45 minutes.

Procedure

The Leader might begin by asking the participants if they would be willing to participate in a guided fantasy experience. If participants are willing, one would begin by instructing them to find a comfortable place in the room and to go there. Each participant is then instructed to sit down and to take a few minutes to relax. The Leader might then suggest that the participants concentrate on their breathing during these few minutes in order to assist them in relaxing.

Then the following general verbal instructions are given:

"I would like you to close your eyes and imagine that you have only one year left to live. You firmly believe that the medical evidence is accurate. Now that you know you will soon die, you decide to sit quietly and review your life. You find an old comfortable rocking chair on a porch or in a room that is so peaceful and quiet and you sit and gently rock. You sit rocking, back and forth, back and forth, back and forth. And as you rock gently back and forth, you remember three different experiences in your life. Each memory comes to you spontaneously, events from your past that you can see so clearly in your mind's eye in detail. With each memory in turn you notice the vivid details. You turn your attention to the first memory and you look very carefully. You notice 1) what you are doing, 2) you see the expression on your face, 3) you notice whether other people are in the memory, 4) if so you notice the expression on their faces and you remember how you felt. *Pause.* You now turn your attention to the second memory and again 1) you notice what you are doing, 2) you see the expression on your face, 3) you notice whether other people are there and if so you see their faces and you can feel how you felt. *Pause.* Now focus on a third and final distinct memory, noticing your behavior and that of any others involved. *Pause.* And as you sit in your rocking chair, rocking back and forth, back and forth, you reflect on your three memories. As you reflect you notice whether the expression in your face in each memory was the same or different. You notice whether you were smiling or laughing or quiet or sad looking. You also reflect on the other people in your memories and you notice if the same people were in each. And as you sit and rock back and forth and reflect on what you were

68

doing in each memory, and the expression on your face, you see what these memories might show about the way you led your life. And you ask yourself whether you are satisfied with these three particular memories as accurately reflecting the best qualities of your life. *Pause. . . .* And as you see what these memories showed, you notice the expression on your face as you continue to rock back and forth, and you notice how you feel."

The facilitator then instructs the participants to continue to imagine rocking and reflecting for a few minutes and to gently return to the present moment as s/he counts slowly from 1 to 10.

Debriefing

1. What was this experience like for you?
2. How clearly were you able to see your memories?
3. What kinds of expressions did you see on your face in each memory? Were you surprised at what you saw?
4. Who were the other people in your memories? What kinds of expressions did you see on their faces? What might this show about the way they felt for you then and now? What might this say about the way you feel about them now?
5. What was happening in your memories? How did you feel about how each memory turned out. . . . pleased? satisfied? embarrassed? hurt? disappointed?
6. Did each memory turn out about the same or different?
7. After you had reviewed all three memories/and you were sitting in your rocking chair rocking, what kind of expression did you see on your face then? How satisfied are you now with these three memories as accurately reflecting the best qualities of your life so far?
8. How might your memories be related to how accepting you now are towards the inevitability of the deaths of those you love? Towards your own death?

35. "Same Time Next Year?"

Goals

1. To experience planning life with a specific identified end.
2. To examine life as it is presently lived in contrast to "planned" life.
3. To examine life as told through obituary statistics.
4. To personalize funeral planning.

This exercise is designed to provide the participant with an opportunity for examination and reflection on his/her own life and some element of control over the environment, relationships and activities at its end and immediately following.

Materials Paper and pen/pencils.

Time 1 to 1.5 hours.

Procedures

Facilitator informs the participants, "You have a terminal illness which cannot be cured by surgery, medication or other treatment. You have been told you have approximately one year to live." Individually answer the following questions after giving some thought to each.

1. How do you intend to spend the last year of your life? Be as specific as you can, including people, places, activities. (Allow about 15 minutes).
2. Write your own obituary notice, including the following:
   a. Cite the usual vital statistics found in an obituary such as name, age, marital status, relatives, etc.
   b. Identify jobs you've had and organizations you have belonged to, with positions you have held in them.
   c. Notable contributions you have made to the community.
   d. Your wishes for memorial tributes from friends.
   e. Would you include a picture? What kind? (Allow another 10-15 minutes).
3. Plan your own funeral including type of visitation and funeral, music selections, flowers, readings and type of disposition (burial, cremation, or entombment). Be specific in identifying these and include them if possible.

Allow about 30 minutes for this third segment followed by optional sharing, and discussion.

Debriefing

1. Did you imagine yourself with a specific illness? What were the physical, mental effects?
2. Did the effects of illness influence your planning?
3. Who and what did you include in your last year?
4. Was this a radical change from the way you now live? If so, why don't you make these changes now?
5. What things, other than those included in your obituary notice, would you want others to know about you?
6. What items in the obituary notice do you see as most significant, least significant? Why?
7. Explain why you chose the specific parts of your funeral. What significance do these things have to you? To others who would be present at your funeral?
8. What will those at your funeral do immediately afterwards?
9. What part of this exercise was easiest? Most difficult?
10. Have you already thought about any of these things? Communicated them to others?
11. Did your feelings change from the beginning of this exercise to the end? In what way?

36. Saying the Last Goodbye

Goals

1. To assist participants in gaining deeper levels of awareness about one aspect of the dying process: leaving loved ones.

2. To provide a structure whereby participants can explore their own current feelings of love and caring for the special people in their lives.

Whether it is dealt with directly or indirectly, dying involves saying goodbye to the people we love. While we can think about saying goodbye, it gives us only an abstract awareness of how we might actually feel to leave those people we care most about. A much deeper level of awareness can be reached by actually verbalizing our goodbyes, as we search for the words, voice tone and tempo that would capture the depth of feeling associated with that experience.

Setting

A quiet, safe environment where participants can feel free to openly explore and discuss their thoughts and emotional reactions.

Time   Approximately 2 hours.

Procedures

This exercise may stir up fairly intense emotional reactions for some participants. The Leader might therefore take initial time to talk about the "OK-ness" of experiencing and expressing feelings. You need also to allow sufficient time at the end of the exercise for adequate debriefing and discussion. One should mention that members can opt out of it if they wish.

1. The Leader asks participants to pair up in dyads. The dyads are then asked to find a place in the room where they each can converse comfortably without undue interference from others.

2. Then they are asked to close their eyes and imagine which five people they would want most to say goodbye to if they knew they would soon be taking a trip that would take them away for a lifetime.

3. Each participant is then asked to write down the names of each of the five people.

4. The participants are then given the following general instructions:

   "Spend a few minutes thinking about the first person on your list. See if you can make a very vivid picture of this person's face in your mind's eye. Allow yourself to remember in rich detail some of the different experiences you've shared with this person. As you remember different experiences, pick one in particular that stands out in your memory. Take a close look at this memory. As you look closely, ask yourself: "What have I learned about living from this person". Take a few minutes to ponder this question and then write down your answer." Then proceed to the next person on your list and go through the same steps until you have a statement of what you've learned about living from each of the five persons on your list.

5. After each participant has completed this, the Leader then gives the following general instructions to each of the dyads.

   "Sit directly across from your partner. Take the first person on your list and imagine your partner is that person. Describe to your partner, as if you were talking directly to the person on your list, the particular experience you recalled. Describe this experience as vividly as you can. Take time to describe what makes the experience important to you. As a closing farewell, then verbalize with tone of voice and tempo that is congruent with your feelings:

'As a reminder of the special times we've shared together, I leave you with this lesson of living I've learned from you . . . (Describe what you have learned). Thank you. Goodbye."

6. The Leader asks the participants to pause here and reflect on the feelings that emerge from this experience.

7. The Leader then instructs partners in the dyads to switch roles and follow the same steps until each member of the dyad has described experiences and "lessons about life" for each of the people on their list.

At the conclusion of the exercise the Leader might ask the entire group of participants to form a close circle to debrief the experience.

Debriefing

1. What was this experience like for you?
2. What kind of feelings were stirred up for you by this experience?
3. What were some of the "lessons of life" that you have learned from the special people in your lives?
4. What was it like for you to verbalize what you have learned and to thank them? To say goodbye?
5. How do you now feel about the five people on your list?
6. What other reactions did you have to this experience?

37. Societal Mortality — Societal Belief*

Goals

To develop the relationship between mortality and belief systems and examine the part death plays in a society's orientation toward life.

Materials   Large sheets of paper, markers and tape, blackboard or overhead projector.

Time   30 to 40 minutes.

Procedures

Subdivide group into three sections with one person in each group assigned the role of recorder/reporter. Assign one of the following sets of societal characteristics to each group.

		Crude Death Rate	Infant Mortality	Longest Life Span
Society A	Urban, Industrial	10 1000	1%	70+
Society B	Agricultural, transitional	30 1000	25%	45 Approx.
Society C	Primitive Agricultural, Hunting Gathering	50 1000	35%	30 or less

The facilitator should distinguish 50/1000 death rate, 35% infant mortality and life expectancy of less than 30 years as "high mortality" and 10/1000 life expectancy of 70+ years as "low mortality" rates.

At this point, instruct each group to answer the following questions about its society in 20 minutes.

1. What age group is most likely to die in this country?
2. How much certainty is there in this society that a person is likely to live his/her entire life span?
3. What general type of belief system do you think would be used by this society to explain death?
4. What influence do you think death has on daily life and activities in this society?
5. What types of social, economic and interpersonal relationships do you think are predominant in this society?

Each group should make a consensus summary/summary statement about its society which recorder/reporter will document and report to the total group. The consensus summary statements can be written out and displayed for all to see. The total group can then compare the statement and analyze elements which lead to their conclusions.

Debriefing

1. Which society would you prefer to live in? to die in? Are they different?
2. How would life be different in each of the other societies?
3. What are the advantages of your society? Disadvantages?
4. Does mortality have an effect on belief systems of societies? What different combinations of data might have a different effect on your society?

---

*Suggested by Steve Steele, Anne Arundel (MD.), Community College.

38. Terminal Illness

Goals

1. To acquaint the individual with some aspects of the experience of terminal illness.
2. To acquaint the individual with some aspects of being with one who is terminally ill.
3. To sensitize the individual to their style of coping with stress.
4. To sensitize the individual to ways s/he might increase or decrease the isolation of a dying person.

Setting

Room large enough to enable all to sit on the floor in pairs.

Materials   One large cushion for every two participants.

Time   45-60 minutes.

Procedures

Each participant selects another participant that s/he likes and trusts. Members of each dyad thus formed face each other approximately 1-2 feet apart. A large cushion is placed between them. Each dyad decides which member will be active and which member will be the guide. The active member is instructed to stand on one foot, bending the knee of the *supporting* leg, and keeping the other foot from touching the floor. The active member should use the guide to maintain balance but *not* to support their weight in any manner. The task of the active member is to remain standing on one leg until that leg gives way and s/he falls onto the cushion. S/he is instructed not to fall through loss of balance and not to elect to fall before their leg gives way on its own through fatigue.

The tasks of the guide are to assure that the active member does not fall through loss of balance, to remind the active member of the task, and to be of whatever assistance s/he can to the active member short of helping to support their weight. After the active member falls, the two members of the dyad exchange roles, the active member now serving as guide and vice versa.

Certain focusing remarks on the part of the instructor can be offered while the dyads are engaging in the exercise. These include asking the active members simply to notice their breathing or their tendency toward laughter, and reminding guides and active members of their respective tasks. Time should be called after 15 minutes each round.

These points are worth bearing in mind as you conduct this SLE:

a. The use of large pillows is an important precaution in order to break the fall of the participants.
b. Participants should be cautioned that those with a heart condition, respiratory difficulties, arthritis, or other illness must use discretion in deciding whether or not to participate.
c. Coping styles will be broadly divergent. The impact of the debriefing process will be maximized if each of these styles is validated and value is placed upon *extending* rather than altering the individual's repertoire of coping responses.
d. It is crucial to avoid using this experience as an initial or early one in the life of a learning group. It is probably used best only with an ongoing, intact membership, and only after they have spent some time together.

Debriefing

The following questions are suggested for inquiry:

a. What was the experience like for you?
b. What were you experiencing as the active person? As the guide?
c. As the active member, what were you feeling toward your guide? Toward the other active members? Toward the Leaders?
d. What did you do with your feelings?
e. How did you use your guide?
f. What did you learn about your style of coping with stress?
g. Do your means of coping include other people? How?
h. What did your guide do that was particularly helpful?
i. What would you have liked from your guide that you did not get?
j. If you did not feel free to ask for it, what got in your way?
k. As the guide, what were you feeling about the situation? About the person you were guiding?
l. Did you feel free to ask that person what would be helpful to him/her? If not, what got in your way?
m. Did you allow your leg to give out or did you fall prematurely?
n. Did you fall? How did you feel about falling?
o. Did it make a difference to go first or second?

39. Time Runs Out

Goals

1. To increase sensitivity to the fact that loss and death can occur without warning.
2. To develop increased awareness of the finiteness of time we have available in our lives.
3. To assist participants in identifying feelings associated with loss and change.

Often we take for granted the amount of time we have available to us in our lives, just as if we have all the time in the world. A personal tragedy or a near fatal accident can shock us into awareness that our time is indeed limited. This awareness can often serve to motivate us to engage our energies more fully in living.

Materials

1. An alarm clock.
2. Some type of construction material for each participant, such as construction paper, cardboard and masking tape, or match sticks and glue.
3. Slips of paper to identify the name of each participant and a container in which to place these.
4. Sheets of paper listing one of the following instructions:
    a. "Your time has run out. All construction materials will be taken from you immediately. Sit quietly for the remainder of the period." (Approximately 1/4 of instruction sheets would contain this specific instruction.)
    b. "You have suffered a serious setback. 1/2 of your construction materials will be taken from you immediately." (Approximately 1/4 of instruction sheets would contain this specific instruction.)
    c. "You have been diagnosed with a terminal illness. You have only two remaining minutes to complete your project." (Approximately 1/4 of instruction sheets would contain this instruction.)
    d. "Due to advancing age, you can no longer complete the project you chose initially. Lower your expectations and choose another project." (Approximately 1/4 of instruction sheets would contain this instruction.)

The Leader would fold sheets and place them in random order in a pile. Total number of sheets would equal total number of participants. Throughout the exercise these instructions are referred to as "Fate" instructions.

Time   1.5 hours.

Procedures

The following exercise is designed to stimulate exploration, discussion and increased awareness about the arbitrary nature of time. In the exercise, the participants are asked to work on a project of their own creation for a period of 30 minutes. During this 30 minute period, an alarm clock is arranged to ring at random intervals. Each time the alarm rings, one of the participant's names is randomly drawn from a "hat" or container. The participant is then required to face one of four possible consequences that is randomly selected:

1. To immediately stop working on the project.
2. To lose 1/2 of his/her construction materials.
3. To have only two remaining minutes to complete the project, or
4. To choose another project task.

By the end of the 30 minute period, at least 3/4 of the participants will have to face a "consequence" that will significantly affect their ability to complete their project as initially planned. The Leader then assists the participants in discussing parallels between this exercise and real life experiences associated with death, loss and aging.

1. Each participant is first given some construction material with the following instruction:

   "During the next 30 minutes each of you will have the opportunity to make something creative out of the construction materials I've just given to you. Your specific task will be to make something that represents a part of yourself that you are proud of. Reflect for a few moments and then choose some specific thing you could make that would represent some aspect of yourself that you feel good about. For example, if you are proud of your ability to make friends, you might make something from the construction materials that symbolizes "friendship.""

   "Do the very best job you can during this next 30 minutes. During this work period, work silently. At random intervals during this 30 minute period, this alarm clock will be set to ring. Each time it rings, I will first randomly draw one of your names from this container. Second, I will randomly select a specific "instruction" for you to follow from this other pile. These instructions are called "Fate Instructions." When the alarm clock rings, continue to work silently on your project unless I come and tap you on the shoulder. If you are tapped on the shoulder, you will be given your specific "Fate" instructions to follow. Please follow these "Fate" instructions and proceed silently."

2. The facilitator then asks each participant to announce to the others what specific construction project they had chosen, and then instructs the participants to begin working.

3. The alarm clock is set to ring at random intervals. During the 30 minute work period, you might arrange for the alarm clock to ring enough times to draw the names of at least 3 to 4 of the participants.

4. When the alarm clock rings, the Leader does the following:
   a. Randomly draws one of the participant's names from the container.
   b. At the same time, s/he randomly selects one of the "Fate" instruction sheets.

The Leader then reads silently the "Fate" instructions, then gives the instruction sheet to the selected participant after first tapping that participant on the shoulder. For example, one might randomly select a "Fate" instruction sheet that stated: "Your time has run out. All construction materials will be taken from you immediately. Sit quietly for the remainder of the period." The Leader would then take the instructions to the selected participant, show the instructions and silently take the construction materials from the participant.

5. S/he would then re-set the alarm clock to ring at some random work period. Again, it is suggested that the Leader set the alarm clock so that it will ring enough times to draw the names of at least 3-4 of the participants.

6. At the conclusion of the 30 minute period, the Leader would ask all the participants to stop working and invite them to discuss their reactions to the experience.

Debriefing

A. One might begin the debriefing procedure by asking each participant to show and describe how much they were able to complete of their individual construction projects. This will encourage the open expression of feelings from the participants. Some possible questions for use in discussing the experience follow:

1. What was this experience like for you?
2. What kind of feelings were stirred up inside you each time the alarm clock rang? When the Leader tapped you on your shoulder? When you read your instructions? As you followed your instructions?
3. What kind of reactions did you have towards the Leader? Toward other participants?

4. Which "Fate" instructions do you believe were most difficult to follow? Why?
5. How might the other participants have assisted you in dealing with your "Fate" instructions, if they had been given the opportunity?
6. How do you feel about the overall quality of your work on your construction project? How might you have improved the quality of your work?
7. For those of you who experienced "setbacks" or who were cut short of time, what were your reactions? How did you deal with these reactions?
8. What are some ways the feelings stirred up in this experience for you might be similar/dissimilar to the feelings a person might have towards some real life experiences such as death, loss and aging?

B. In order to extend the learning parallel between this simulated exercise and death, the Leader might close the exercise thus,

1. S/he would request that each person, in turn, bring their created projects to the center of the room. Each person would place their project on the floor and then return to be seated in the circle. As each person returned to their seat the Leader might perform a "Ritual" of covering the "Created Project" with a box or blanket and then destroying the remains of the project. The Leader would explain that each project was to be destroyed and each participant had the option of looking on or turning his head away. After destroying each project, the Leader might then debrief this part of the exercise with the following questions:

   a. What was it like for you to give up your project? To hear that it had to be destroyed?
   b. When you learned your project was to be destroyed, what thoughts did you have about whether to watch or turn your head away? How did you decide which to do?
   c. What kind of feelings did you then have about seeing your project destroyed? What feelings came later?
   d. What kind of feelings did you have about seeing other's projects destroyed?
   e. What kind of learning did this part of the experience provide you?

40. Trip to the Cemetery

Goals

1. To expose individuals to the inevitability of their own deaths.
2. To invite participants to confront the mortality and ultimate disposition of their bodies.
3. To permit them to make a symbolic statement about their uniqueness.

Setting

A moderately large cemetery with varied terrain and vegetation.

Time   2-3 hours.

Procedure

Preparation:

a. It is recommended that this exercise be combined with the exercise entitled "Eulogy" and/or "Planning the Last Day". If this is done, participants should have written their own eulogies prior to the trip to the cemetery, and should have these in hand during the visit.
b. The facilitator should have secured permission for the visit from the cemetery management prior to the trip.
c. Participants should be instructed to meet at the cemetery at a designated time and place. It is suggested that each participant come alone in order to permit anticipatory thoughts and feelings about the experience to emerge with minimal intrusion and diffusion.

Instructions:

After all participants have arrived, the group is presented with the following guidelines:

"Take the next 30 minutes to be alone and explore the grounds of the cemetery. Keep the quiet, give yourself a chance to reflect and respect the privacy of other individuals and groups, whether they be fellow participants or strangers. Allow yourself to pursue any feelings, thoughts, or images that come to mind. Do not push them away; experience them fully.

During your walk, find a spot which especially appeals to you and in which you feel particularly comfortable. Spend a few minutes in that place, attending to how it feels to sit there and thinking about how *you* are represented by the place you have selected.

After you have taken some time to explore the grounds and to spend some time in a special spot of your choosing, return here (to the designated meeting place) and we will talk for a few minutes before moving on to the next part of the experience."

When participants re-convene at this point, some minimal (no more than 5-10 minutes) discussion is appropriate. The objective is simply to "touch base" with participants and make a cursory determination of how each is being affected by the experience thus far.

Participants remain together for the next portion of the visit. Each participant in turn leads the group to the spot he or she has selected as being of special importance. The participant who has selected that spot takes a few moments to share why that place was selected and in what ways it reflects the individual who chose it. If the eulogy is included in this exercise, the participant then gives his or her own eulogy to another participant to read. (See procedure in "Eulogy" page 53 for description of this segment.)

The group moves in turn to the place selected by each participant, giving every person the opportunity (a) to describe the significance of having selected that spot and (b) to hear his or her own eulogy read aloud by another individual of the participant's choosing.

Although it is neither realistic nor desirable to prevent participants from sharing their reactions as they move one place to the next, extensive debriefing of this activity should be reserved until the group has visited each participant's place in the cemetery.

Debriefing

The trip to the cemetery tends to promote introspection, a sense of quietness, and an appreciation of one's ultimate aloneness. The result is that there might exist among the participants a disinclination to discuss the experience in detail and a preference for silent reflection within the supportive context of the group. Such withdrawal should not be viewed as undesirable, though some discussion should be encouraged in the following manner:

Participants should be *offered* the opportunity to articulate their reactions. The facilitator can provide this opportunity by respecting participants' rights to privacy, maintaining an atmosphere of warmth and safety, validating the full range of participant reactions, modeling appropriate self-disclosure, and remaining attentive and responsive to individuals' needs.

The following are some of the reactions that might be anticipated:
a. memories of deaths/funerals of loved ones
b. anticipation of the reactions of loved ones to the participant's death
c. meditation upon infiniteness of a "final resting place"
d. sadness about one's own death or the deaths of others
e. fear/anxiety about one's own death or the deaths of others
f. contemplation of one's body, its finiteness, its disposition
g. speculation about mortality and immortality
h. reflection upon one's life and that which has lent it meaning

III.   Instrumental Exercises and Applied Designs

This section is a short collection of forms and SLEs requiring some written stimuli. They represent a range of affective demands, but all are designed to enable the participants to reflect on their lifestyles in some way, and to attempt a resynthesis and reconciliation of past personal events with the prospects for an altered future. Selection of these requires a knowledge of the group members' willingness and capability for a thorough discussion of the material generated — a must for these SLEs no less than in the previous section.

41. Certifying Life!

Goals

1. To provide a projective experience that enables people to reflect on their versions of personally appropriate or probable deathstyles.
2. To expose individuals to a pertinent medico-legal document, its purposes and content as an educational consideration.

Materials

A copy of the local (state) form (or next page if unavailable) certifying death, reproduced in sufficient numbers for all participants, a pencil/pen.

Time

Approximately 30 minutes to instruct and complete, then another 45 minutes to debrief.

Procedures

This is a commonly used tool for enabling people to clarify their attitudes and to envision some scenarios for their deaths and "dying trajectories" as Glaser & Straus called them.

There are several ways to use the "instrument." Briefly, the certificate can be introduced as "... a once-in-a-lifetime experience. The next time your name appears on this kind of document, you'll not be able to read or contemplate it — you'll be dead. And, your freedom of choice for the exercise here won't exist then!"

Following that introduction, the facilitator shares the goals of the SLE, and distributes the forms. Then s/he quickly touches on each of the lines and categories to be completed, explaining each where the meaning is not literal. Then, the participants are to complete the death certificate, after which discussion and sharing of responses proceeds.

Variations

This exercise can be given as a "homework" assignment, then debriefed in the next meeting. Or, it can be varied by asking the group to think first of a living loved one, then to fill it out for *them* as they think/hope death might occur. Or, they can fill it out either as "expected" or "hoped for" either using self or significant other as decedent.

The latter variations pose some difficulty at times, as thoughts of children particularly are met with understandable resistance due to some "magical thinking" fears, and superstitions. Also, at times some participants balk at even their own certificate, as that too engenders some fearful concerns. The facilitator must be aware of such responses, and must allow for wide latitude and even non-responding behavior from some.

Debriefing

This SLE seems best approached first as a personal statement of "lifestyle" and "legacy". Then, discussion and sharing of responses can be more readily undertaken.

Re: "lifestyle", questions such as these may be useful to ponder:

What does your choice of time (age) and mode of death say to you about your ways of living, your way of dying/your implicit plans for future? (Or the *other* if not a personal certificate).

CERTIFICATE OF DEATH

LOCAL FILE NUMBER   STATE FILE NUMBER

DECEDENT

DECEASED — FIRST NAME	MIDDLE	LAST	SEX	DATE OF DEATH (Month, day, year)
1.			2.	3.

RACE — White, Black, American Indian, Etc. (Specify)	AGE — LAST BIRTHDAY (Years)	UNDER 1 YEAR		UNDER 1 DAY		DATE OF BIRTH (Month, day, year)	CITY, TOWN, OR LOCATION OF DEATH
		MOS	DAYS	HOURS	MIN.		
4.	5a.	5b.		5c.		6.	7a.

7a _ _ _ _ _

HOSPITAL OR OTHER INSTITUTION — NAME (If not in either, give street and number)	WAS DECEDENT EVER IN U.S. ARMED FORCES? (Specify Yes or No) NAME WAR
7b.	8.

7b _ _ _ _ _

CITY, TOWN STATE, OF BIRTH (if not in U.S.A name country)	CITIZEN OF WHAT COUNTRY	MARRIED, NEVER MARRIED, WIDOWED, DIVORCED (Specify)	SPOUSE (if wife, give maiden name)
9a.	9b.	10.	11.

SOCIAL SECURITY NUMBER	USUAL OCCUPATION (Give kind of work done during most of working life, even if retired)	KIND OF BUSINESS OR INDUSTRY
12.	13a.	13b.

14 _ _ _ _ _

MAILING ADDRESS OF RESIDENCE STREET OR R.F.D. AND NUMBER, CITY OR TOWN, STATE, ZIP CODE	CITY OR TOWN OF RESIDENCE (if different from mailing address)
14a.	14b.

CT _ _ _ _ _

PARENTS

FATHER — FIRST NAME	MIDDLE	LAST	MOTHER — FIRST NAME	MIDDLE	MAIDEN NAME
15.			16.		

INFORMANT — NAME	MAILING ADDRESS (Street or R.F.D No., city or town, state, zip)
17a.	17b.

DISPOSITION

BURIAL, CREMATION, REMOVAL, OTHER (Specify)	CEMETERY OR CREMATORY — NAME AND LOCATION	CITY OR TOWN STATE
18a.	18b.	

FUNERAL DIRECTOR — LICENSEE (Signature)	FUNERAL HOME — NAME AND ADDRESS (Street or R.F.D. no. city or town, state, zip)
19a.	19b.

CERTIFIER

To be Completed by CERTIFYING PHYSICIAN Only

To the best of my knowledge, death occurred at the time, date and place and due to the cause(s) stated	DEGREE OR TITLE	DATE SIGNED (Month, day, year)	HOUR OF DEATH
20a. (Signature)		20b.	20c. M

NAME AND ADDRESS OF CERTIFIER (Type or print)	WAS DEATH REFERRED TO MEDICAL EXAMINER (Specify Yes or No)	IF HOSP. OR INST. Indicate DOA. OP/Emer Rm., Inpatient (Specify)
20d.	21a.	21b.

NAME AND ADDRESS OF ATTENDING PHYSICIAN IF OTHER THAN CERTIFIER (Type or Print)	LENGTH OF ATTENDANCE (Specify) (Hrs., wks., mo., yrs.)
22.	23.

REGISTRAR

REGISTRAR	DATE RECEIVED BY REGISTRAR (Mo., day, yr.)
24a. (Signature)	24b.

CAUSE OF DEATH

25

PART I   IMMEDIATE CAUSE   (ENTER ONLY ONE CAUSE PER LINE FOR (a), (b), AND (c).)

	Interval between onset and death
(a)	
DUE TO, OR AS A CONSEQUENCE OF: (Intermediate cause)	Interval between onset and death
(b)	
DUE TO, OR AS A CONSEQUENCE OF: (Underlying cause)	Interval between onset and death
(c)	

PART II OTHER SIGNIFICANT CONDITIONS — Conditions contributing to death but not related to cause given in PART I (a)	AUTOPSY (Yes or No)	If yes were findings considered in determining cause of death
	26a.	26b.

ACCIDENT (Specify Yes or No)	DATE OF INJURY (Mo ,day, yr)	HOUR OF INJURY	DESCRIBE HOW INJURY OCCURRED
27a.	27b.	27c. M	27d.

INJURY AT WORK (Specify Yes or No)	PLACE OF INJURY At home, farm, street, factory, office building, etc (Specify)	LOCATION STREET OR R.F.D NO CITY OR TOWN STATE
27e.	27f.	27g.

BRIEF INSTRUCTIONS ON REVERSE SIDE

Law requires Funeral Director to file this certificate with the City or Town Clerk at the Place of Death within 7 days

---

BURIAL-TRANSIT PERMIT

DEPARTMENT OF HEALTH   PERMIT NUMBER

PERMIT MUST Accompany Remains to DESTINATION

DECEASED — Name FIRST	MIDDLE	LAST	SEX	DATE OF DEATH (Month, day, year)

RACE	AGE	PLACE OF DEATH (City or town, state)

BURIAL, CREMATION, REMOVAL OTHER (Specify)	CEMETERY OR CREMATORY NAME AND LOCATION CITY OR TOWN STATE

FUNERAL DIRECTOR — LICENSEE (Signature)	FUNERAL HOME — Name and Address (Street or R.F.D. no., city or town, state, zip)

SEXTON must return permit to City or Town Clerk at Place of Disposal on Fifth of Next Month

CERTIFICATION: I certify that death occurred from Natural causes (see over), that referral to the Medical Examiner is **not** required, and that permission is hereby granted to dispose of this body

Signature of certifying Physician	Degree or title	Date signed

Authorized disposition as stated above occurred on (Date)	Tomb	Lot	Signature of Sexton or Person in Charge of Cemetery

THIS PERMIT VALID ONLY IF SIGNED BOTH BY PHYSICIAN AND BY FUNERAL DIRECTOR   SEE OTHER SIDE

83

TYPE OR PRINT ALL ENTRIES IN PERMANENT DARK (PREFERABLY BLACK) INK

FUNERAL DIRECTOR:

Item 1 — Capitalize each letter of surname. Enter full middle name (i.e., Jane Anne JONES)

Item 6 — Enter first three letters of month of birth (i.e., Jan., Feb., Mar., etc.)

Items 5 & 6 — If decendent was more than one year old, enter only completed years (5a).
If decedent was more than one day but less than one year old, enter only completed months or days (5b).
If decedent was under one day old, enter hours or minutes (5c). Check age against birthdate (Item 6).

Item 7b — For deaths not occurring in a hospital or institution, enter full street address.

Items 10 & 11 — Name of spouse should be entered only if Item 10 is "married" or "widowed." (Separated individuals are legally married and should be so reported: name of spouse should be entered).

Item 13 — Enter occupation followed during most of life; "retired" is **not** an acceptable entry.

Item 14 — For residents of institutions, enter residence address prior to admission to institution unless the decedent was a long-term resident of the institution and no longer maintains his former residence.

CERTIFYING PHYSICIAN:

The physician is responsible for completing the date of death, the "Certification" and "Cause of Death" sections.

Item 3 — Enter first three letters of month of death (i.e., Jan., Feb., Mar., etc.).

Item 23 — Length of attendance refers to the length of time the attending physician had attended the deceased and should be expressed as a number with the highest unit.

Item 25 — Cause of Death. In Part I, please give the sequence of events that led to death, specifying the underlying cause on the lowest-used line. Part II is used to report other important diseases or conditions, if any, that contributed to death but were not related to the immediate cause (Ia). When autopsy findings differ significantly from clinical findings originally certified, send the State Registrar a supplementary report (Form VS 218).

To reduce the need for querying physicians on certain causes of death, please note the following suggestions:

A. **Pneumonia.** Indicate as "primary" or specify the underlying cause on the line below.
B. **Malignant Neoplasms.** Enter the primary site of a malignancy, or state that the primary site is unknown. Always qualify tumors as benign, malignant, or unknown whether benign or malignant.
C. **Symptoms, Ill-defined, and Terminal Conditions** that seldom arise independently are unsatisfactory for certification if the underlying cause is known. If the underlying cause is unknown, please so state.
   A qualifying phrase such as "probably" may be used where the diagnosis is uncertain or unconfirmed.

FORM REQUIRED BY GENERAL LAWS (Sec. 23-3-16)

PHYSICANS — Refer the death to the Medical Examiner IF:
Death is due to, or there is a suspicion of, trauma of any nature;
Death is sudden in a public place;
Death is from a drug or toxic substance;
Death is sudden and the patient has not been attended by a physician;
Death is from an infection capable of causing an epidemic;
Death is related to job, work place, or the environment;
Death occurs within 24 hours of hospitalization or ER care;
Death occurs during or immediately after surgery or diagnostic or therapeutic procedure.

FUNERAL DIRECTORS: The burial-transit permit is required for any manner of disposition of a dead body, including interment, storage, cremation, and transportation. A certificate of cremation must also be obtained from the medical examiner for any body which is to be cremated.

When used as a transit permit for transportation by common carrier, this permit or a duplicate thereof should be enclosed in a strong envelope attached to the shipping case. No separate transit permit is required.

Before shipment by train or express, the body must be embalmed; or if this is not practicable, must be enclosed in a tightly sealed outer case.

SEXTON: It is unlawful for any sexton, or other person in charge of a burial place, to permit burial or other disposition of a dead body before a burial-transit permit is deposited with him.

all permits must be preserved and forwarded to the City or Town Clerk where the burial takes place on the fifth day of the month next succeeding.

Re: "Legacy", this kind of direction may be worth pursuing:

What do your choices say will be your survivor's legacies to bereave: (a) emotionally (b) physically (c) in terms of economics (d) with respect to their psychosocial loss and reintegration?

With respect to mode of corporal disposition, i.e. burial, cremation, removal for same, what choices and possible difficulties does that present given your understanding of their wishes on this topic?

Several other lines of inquiry can be taken, including some charting of the data for intra-group comparisons. Also, discussion of the impact of completing (or *not* completing) the certificate should be done, with participants sharing their emotional responses to the task or parts of it. This is an essential minimum for debriefing.

References

Kastenbaum, R. and Sabatini, P., "The do-it-yourself death certificate as a research technique." *Life Threatening Behavior*, 1973, 2, 20-32.

42. Coping with Personal Loss

Goals

1. To examine the loss experience of participants
2. To explore the emotional sequelae to reconciled as well as unresolved losses.
3. To discover the growthful aspects of "surviving" significant losses — the "loss-to-gain" phenomenon.
4. To share the means and methods used to cope with varying losses.

Setting

Circular seating with groups of no more than 6-7 per group; subgroups can simultaneously be led.

Materials

A copy of the self-inventory which follows, reproduced in sufficient number for the whole group of participants, plus a pen or pencil for each.

Time

One hour or about 10 minutes for each member of the group. (Note group size limitations recommended above).

Procedures

The leader introduces the SLE as "... an opportunity to examine retrospectively the various loss histories people have experienced." Then distribute the self-inventory and a writing instrument (as needed) to each participant. If the group is larger than six or so, sub-groups of no fewer than four should be arranged. Thus, when the group size exceeds eight, such arrangements are desirable, with the instructions, and later questions in the debriefing phase led by a single overall facilitator.

The discussion of the written responses can take either of two basic formats — with a discussion of each participant's complete responses going on in turn, or, preferably perhaps, a comparable response can be sought from each group member for each of the (three) losses listed. Then, too, another variation involves use of the A, B, and C sections in a manner of orchestrating the loss-to-gain "lessons" for each person. Whatever approach is used, illumination of the goals for this exercise with optimal representation of each group member and with a maximization of the variety of losses and responses to them are the desirable outcomes. The following additional discussion points and questions can also be pursued to some benefit.

Debriefing

1. Did you notice that the nature of the lost object only partially dictates intensity and complexity of the emotional experience that follows? Cite examples.
2. To what extent was the age at loss a critical developmental factor in the loss experience?
3. Is the phenomenon of "psychosocial homeostasis" apparent in many of the cited loss resolution discussions?
4. What were the forms of coping used and how successful with what losses were each of these?
5. How critical has the passage of time proved to be in the loss resolution experience?
6. What experiential lessons can be compared to grief/bereavement theory from this set of discussions?

Self-Inventory: Coping with Personal Loss

A. List the 3 most significant losses you personally sustained in life to date. They don't need to be in any hierarchical order. Could be people, things/objects, hopes, beliefs, attitudes, whatever. Be brief and concrete!

_____
_____
_____
_____

B. In which of the losses above have you completed your grief resolution? How has such resolution moved you to more self-affirmation, creative living, growth? Again, be specific and concise as you write.

_____
_____
_____
_____
_____
_____
_____

C. In which of the three losses noted above have you NOT completed your grieving? In what ways is this manifest in your living today? Be concrete and brief again.

_____
_____
_____
_____
_____
_____
_____

43. Death & Dying: A Brief Personal Inventory

Goals

1. To provide some data for further examination re: some of an individual's perceptions and experiences about dying and death.
2. To identify personal issues and topical interests in this subject matter.
3. To offer a rough gauge for comparing preliminary data and later (in a course) responses to some central topics and viewpoints.

Materials   Copy of inventory on next page plus pencil/pen.

Time   Usually takes 10-20 minutes to complete on own.

Procedures

Aside from an introduction of the exercise, this inventory can be used in a number of ways:

One use is to gather data solely for the facilitator to acquire a knowledge of the range of experiences, beliefs and questions of the participants at an early point in the class/program.

Another use is to give the instrument for completion at the beginning and again at the conclusion of a course or workshop, and to note changes. This presumes a sufficient passage of time for such comparisons to be drawn validly.

Both of the above can be varied additionally by having the participants share their responses with one another, in small groups, or for the total group to participate. Some of the further ways to "read out" and process this SLE follow.

Debriefing

The facilitator who chooses to share the group's answers at some point may use pairs or small groups (4-6 maximum suggested), do some charting of the group's range of responses, particularly on numerically based questions, or even remark on change units where a pre/post format is employed.

Questions useful in "milking" this experience for more than the written responses might center on such issues as:

*   Sources of influence on certain items (parental, cultural, age, religion, etc.)
*   If field trips are employed as part of the course or workshop, those impacts on certain items can be discussed and elaborated at some length
*   Propose assigning subsequent in-depth studies/papers or team presentations on topics or attitudes of common interest or opposite positions.

Dying and Death: A Brief Personal Inventory

Answer the following briefly:

1. Who/When/Under what circumstances did your most recent death experience occur?

2. How many more years do you anticipate at present you will live?

3. What life-threatening or life-endangering behaviors do you engage in? (e.g. fast driving, no seat belts, unwise diet, excessive drinking, smoking, etc.)

4. If you could choose it, where and how would you prefer your death to occur?

5. What is your preferred mode of body disposition at death?

6. My expectations for "afterlife" are:

7. Have you made a *will* yet? If yes, what is the relationship of the primary beneficiary?

8. Cite any bioethical quandaries that you are personally concerned about: (e.g., war, suicide, euthanasia, abortion, etc.)

9. At what age do *you* consider death for a person is no longer "premature"?

10. My (present) questions about death, dying, bereavement and grief are:

44. Life Lines: The View from Now

Goals

1. To enable participants to obtain graphic perspectives on their development to date and future aspirations.
2. To provide a pointed chronicle of the impacts of "signal" events — birth, deaths, losses, gains in people's lives.
3. To similarly afford an opportunity for planning one's "remaining" time as a new perhaps revised future prospect in the face of past events.

Materials

Pencil, pen or, if possible, 2 or 3 differently colored markers for each participant.

Form on the attached page or model on board, or on flipchart the general arrangement of lines and polar labels.

Time

Variable, but 20 to 30 minutes minimum is needed by each person to complete their own chart, and another 30 minutes is desirable to debrief the experience, first in small groups, then in summary with all.

Procedures

Share the goals of this written part of the exercise as above, and then have them proceed for awhile on their own before convening subgroups. Instructions are simply these:

"Using the printed form, first label the key events of your life from birth to this day on top of the first line, while marking the year (and month, if possible) of each just below it. Space them according to some appropriate proportion or distance both in relation to one another temporally, and with overall respect to the total time the line encompasses. These events are those which *you* view as signal or pivotal, important happenings in your past, which had a strong meaning or impact for you." (If using multiple colors, encourage different ones to be used for date and event). (Pause about 15 minutes, and then give the next instructions, or if preferred, these can be given as a continuing part of the preliminary directions above.)

"Once you've filled and labelled the past/top line to your satisfaction, go on to the bottom line, and starting at the extreme right end, date your plausible (hoped for) year of death, then go to the left hand end, and put today's date as on the right above, and proceed in a similar way to label and date your projected future, attending to such fantasies with reasonable spacing. Pay attention, too, to the expected loss events involving marriages of children, deaths of others of importance, and lifestyle changes wished for in that possible future."

An option hereafter, as they complete the second line, is to ask them to go back over each line, and circle the one or two most profound experiences of the past, and the one or two most wanted aspirations of the future. When this is done, a later question for discussion can center on each person's "criteria" for selection.

Debriefing

Usually in pairs or groups of three or four (maximum), the exercise can be debriefed with the following kinds of inquiry directed by the facilitator:

1. How difficult/easy was it to do?
2. Was the experience:
   - enjoyable or painful?
   - enlightening or affirming?
   - something you think of often?
3. What mode of death/dying did you choose for yourself? Why?
4. What prompted your selection of the time for your death?
5. What patterns emerged in reviewing the past, e.g. losses, gains, maturational transformations, etc.?
6. Did you learn anything about yourself or your lifestyle as a part of completing this SLE?
7. The inevitable: If you had it to re-do, what would change? And, related to that, in what ways do you see your projected future as "compensating" for deficits felt in the past?

Life Lines: The View From Now

Birth Date ———————————————————————— **Today's Date**

Today's Date ———————————————————————— **Death Date**

45. Longevity Calculation

Goals

1. To assist participants in predicting how long they might expect to live.
2. To assist participants in identifying specific ways they might increase their chances for living longer.
3. To serve as a stimulus for discussing one's personal reactions to the inevitability of death.

Many of us rarely take the time to make a realistic estimate of how long we might expect to live. This SLE provides a method for predicting life expectancy that is similar to the rationale used by some life insurance companies. This simple exercise may be used as a stimulus to assist individuals in thinking about and acknowledging the inevitability of dying, as well as to focus on ways we might influence how long we actually live.

Materials

Paper or pre-printed form and pencil for each participant.

Time

Varies depending on version used and amount of debriefing; average of 45 minutes.

Procedures

1. The Leader can introduce this exercise by asking the group of participants to imagine how long they expect to live.

2. Then, instruct the participants to go through the following procedure to find how a life insurance actuary would go about predicting their life expectancy.*

   A. Start with seventy-two
   B. *Gender:* If you are male, subtract three. If you are female add four. That's right, there's a seven-year spread between the sexes.
   C. 1. If you live in an urban area with a population over two million, subtract 2. If you live in a town under ten thousand, or on a farm, add 2. City life means pollution, tension.
      2. If you work behind a desk, subtract 3. If your work requires regular, heavy physical labor, add 3.
      3. If you exercise vigorously (tennis, running, swimming, etc.) five times a week for at least a half-hour, add 2.
      4. If you live with a spouse or friend, add 5. If not, subtract 1 for every 10 years alone since age 25. People together eat better, take care of each other, are less depressed.
   D. *Psyche*
      1. Sleep more than 10 hours each night? Subtract 4.
      2. Are you intense, aggresive, easily angered? Subtract 3. Are you easygoing, relaxed, a follower? Add 3.
      3. Are you happy? Add 1. Unhappy? Subtract 2.
      4. Have you had a speeding ticket in the last year? Subtract 1. Accidents are the fourth-largest cause of death; first, in young adults.
   E. *Success*
      1. Earn over $50,000 a year? Subtract 2. Wealth breeds high living, tension.
      2. If you finished college, add 1. If you have a graduate or professional degree, add 2 more. Education seems to lead to moderation; at least that's the theory.
      3. If you are 65 or over and still working, add 3. Retirement kills.

F. *Heredity*
   1. If any grandparent lived to 85, add 2. If all four grandparents lived to eighty, add 6.
   2. If either parent died of stroke or heart attack before the age of 50, subtract 4.
   3. If any parent, brother, sister under 50 has (or had) cancer or a heart condition, or has had diabetes since childhood, subtract 3.
G. *Health*
   1. Smoke more than 2 packs a day? Subtract 8. One or two packs a day? Subtract 6. One-half to one? Subtract 3.
   2. Drink the equivalent of a quarter-bottle of liquor a day? Subtract 1.
   3. Overweight by 50 pounds or more? Subtract 8. By 30 to 50 pounds? Subtract 4. By 10 to 30 pounds? Subtract 2.
   4. Men over 40, if you have annual checkups, add 2. Women, if you see a gynecologist once a year, add 2.
H. *Age Adjustment*
   Between 30 and 40? Add 2. Between 40 and 50? Add 3. Between 50 and 70? Add 4. Over 70? Add 5.

The table below tells what percentage of the population you will outlive, providing you make it to the specified age.

Age	Men	Women
60	26%	15%
65	36%	20%
70	48%	30%
75	61%	39%
80	75%	53%
85	87%	70%
90	96%	88%
95	99%	97%
100	99.9%	99.6%

Variations

There are several versions of this SLE which generally accomplish the same objectives in similar ways. The reader is referred specifically to Schulz, R. *The Psychology of Death, Dying and Bereavement.* Reading, MA.: Addison-Wesley, 1979, and for a more extensive look at lifestyle data, with the adult version of the Life Events Scale built in, one can consult Vickery, D.M., *LifePlan for your health,* Reading, MA.: Addison-Wesley, 1978.

Debriefing

1. What was it like for you to be computing how long you can expect to live?
2. How does the age you arrived at through this computational procedure compare with the age you intuitively imagined prior to the exercise? If there are differences, how do you account for them?
3. Which of the life expectancy criteria seemed to have special relevance for you? Why?
4. If you were to make any adjustments now in your style of living, what would you do? Why?

---

*From Passell, Peter. *How To . . .*, New York: Farrar, Straus, and Giroux, 1976.

46.   Tombstone Epitaph*

Goals

This SLE enables the participant to creatively make a personal statement that reflects their (a) life goals, (b) personal values, (c) vision of immortality.

Materials

A sheet of paper roughly 8½x11 inches with a facsimile of the following filling the page with copies in sufficient numbers for each participant are needed. Also, each person will need a pen, pencil, or marker.

Time: 45 minutes

Procedures

Each participant is given a copy of the "tombstone" with the instructions printed at the bottom. It should be emphasized that "brevity is the soul of wit" and they might be challenged to capture their epitaph in simple, clever and straightforward words, using any form of narrative or verse that would "fit," both literally and symbolically.

Debriefing

As this is basically an exercise involving "projection" — into the future as well as the past — processing of this SLE is best accomplished in ways that maximize the interpretation and understanding of what is being said on each tombstone. Thus, the group can hang all their epitaphs for perusal by the total group, sharing explanations of them one at a time after all tour the "gallery." Or, pairs of participants up to about 8 people (maximum) can alternately elaborate on the meanings and rationale behind their words. Questions might well focus therein on the three major goal areas for this experience, namely how the epitaph represents each person's views of their social and personal values, their future life objectives as currently viewed, and their outlook on personal and specie immortality.

See next page for example of tombstone.

---

*Suggested by Robert Kastenbaum, Boston, Massachusetts.

- - - - - - - - - - - - - - - - - - - -

- - - - - - - - - - - - - - - - - - - -

- - - - - - - - - - - - - - - - - - - -

- - - - - - - - - - - - - - - - - - - -

- - - - - - - - - - - - - - - - - - - -

- - - - - - - - - - - - - - - - - - - -

- - - - - - - - - - - - - - - - - - - -

- - - - - - - - - - - - - - - - - - - -

- - - - - - - - - - - - - - - - - - - -

On the tombstone above, write your name and the
epitaph which you would like to have written on your
monument — in other words, write what you would
like to be remembered for.

IV. Role Plays

This final set of SLEs is a brief collection of role-playing opportunities which are simultaneously the most difficult and potentially the most enriching SLEs to carry out. When used effectively, they can be the most poignant and even profound learning experiences with which one can teach. But, they also are the most demanding on all concerned if well conducted. By all means, some experimenting with combinations of these, and with role playing "coaching" of participants are encouraged.

47. Answering Children's Questions About Death*

Goals

This exercise is designed to:

1. Give participants practice in responding to typical queries children address to adults and older siblings about death and dying.
2. Gain some understanding for the developmental complexity of various ways of responding to different levels of understanding.
3. To get feedback on the *appropriateness, accuracy,* and *comfort* with which one responds to children's questions.

Setting

Room large enough for a single seat amidst a circle of seats adequate for the number of participants, with a recommended maximum of 8-10 per group.

Materials

A set of cards (3 x 5 inch or smaller) with the following age and questions on them in equal numbers to the total of the group. Examples follow:

- 5 year old: "Where is 'dead'?"
- 6 year old: "Will I die when I am old too?"
- 7 year old: "Will I ever see Grandpa again?" (question asked after burial of grandfather)
- 7 year old: "Don't people die when they go to the hospital?"
- 4 year old: "It's only 'bad guys' who get killed. . .right?"
- 13 year old: "I'll never get over her death, will you?" (speaking of a peer's death)
- 8 year old: "Was Mommy angry with me? She didn't say good-bye when she died."
- 9 year old: "What happens when a person is burned up?" (cremated)
- 6 year old: "Can you tell me what happens when a person dies? Do they go to heaven or hell or what?"
- 15 year old: "Why didn't Dad want to go on living?"

Time

Five minutes per group member plus 20 minutes to debrief at the end.

Procedures

A. The group is gathered in a circle with a chair in the center for each "child" to be portrayed.
B. Each participant is given a card in turn which has the question they are to ask and elaborate on briefly, and a notation of the age of the questioner.
C. Randomly, each group member selects one of the outer circle members to be the respondent. (The leader may stipulate that no one person be called on more than once or twice.)
D. The question and role-play exchange should not exceed three minutes each, with the respondent becoming the next role player/child.

---

*Suggested by: Michael R. Slavit, Austin, TX.

E. At the end of each Q & A segment, the remainder of the group is to comment in critique on the respondent's answer along the dimensions of:
- appropriateness (developmentally)
- accuracy (validity of response)
- comfort (exhibited while responding; verbal and non-verbal)

F. After the entire group has had their turn at each role once, the group facilitator leads some summary discussion of the impact of such an exercise.

Debriefing

1. How did the experience of being asked these questions by a "young person" strike you?
2. Which role was easier? Why?
3. Did you draw on past experiences either in asking or answering questions after you began the role-play?
4. Did you give specific identity to others when answering the question?
5. Did your anxiety level increase or decrease after the initial exchange as the role play developed?
6. What developmental differences did you notice? How did answers change depending on developmental level? How did questioning change?
7. Was your role as answerer affected by your role as questioner?
8. What other questions would you think appropriate?
9. Are these also questions that might be asked by adults?
10. Did this exercise help you? Why or why not?

48. Potlatch

Goals

To design and experience a potlatch and its life/death values. Participants will examine individual and group values, symbols and attitudes toward death and the cultural and communal aspects of rituals related to death and dying.

Materials

First Session: dictionary, paper, pencil, books which define a potlatch.
Second Session: paper, pencils, and pens.
Third Session: any materials identified in the second session.

Time Three forty-minute sessions.

Procedures

First Session: is divided into three segments. The first 15-20 minutes should be devoted to individual research. Participants will use a variety of materials to gather information on a potlatch and take notes. This can also be done prior to the session with notes brought by each participant. In the second segment (15 minutes), participants will share findings and (third) break into groups of 8 to 12 which will work together in the next session.

Second Session: Participants work in their groups for the purpose of designing a potlatch. To do this the group members will need to identify attitudes, symbols, roles and rituals and their significance. By the end of this session each person in the group should have an identified role in the potlatch presentation and the group should have identified a list of materials needed for the presentation and know who will provide them.

Third Session: It is often best to have this session after a lapse of several days which will allow group members to do additional planning and also allow each individual to examine his or her role in the potlatch. At this session each small group will present a potlatch for the entire group and answer any questions about their presentation; also they will discuss the exercise.

For the first session it is important to have a variety of materials available so that each participant may do research using several resources. Although there may be duplicated material, a variety of both descriptions and definitions is important. This activity may be done in relation to any study of culture, social studies or any course which covers ritual, custom, symbols or values.

Debriefing

1. Do you like the custom of the potlatch?
2. What were the characteristics of the culture you portrayed?
3. What attitudes toward death were expressed?
4. What attitudes toward life were expressed?
5. What, if any, similar rituals exist in your culture or background?
6. How did your understanding of a potlatch differ from the first session to the third?

49. Role Playing Situations: Issues Relating to Death, Loss and Separation

Goals

1. To assist students in gaining insight into how they might feel and respond to a situation associated with death and loss.
2. To assist students in recognizing that there are wide variations in feelings, responses, and interactions for each situation.

Role playing exercises provide the opportunity to examine feelings, attitudes, and thoughts about a situation prior to actually having to deal with the situation. Participants have a chance to gain an experiential understanding, explore options, and examine responses to potentially impactful situations within a structure that provides opportunity for discussion and insight. Role playing exercises are particularly useful in assisting students in gaining more than just an "intellectual" understanding by integrating the cognitive and affective dimensions of the learning exercise. Consequently, these exercises can be particularly effective teaching tools for instruction in the area of death and loss.

Materials

1. Instruction sheets describing the individual roles to be played.
2. Information sheet listing constructive guidelines for role-playing, as follows.
3. Name tags and markers.

Time   One to two hours.

Procedures

Because role play situations are enacted in the first person and have a "here-and-now" focus, the level of emotional involvement for the participants can become quite intense. The leader should insure that participation is voluntary and that participants can feel free to end the role playing exercises at any time.

1. The leader gives a rationale for the value of role playing exercises. S/he then distributes "Tips for Role Playing" for participants and discusses these prior to beginning the role plays.
2. Participants who volunteer to play the roles are given an envelope or index card that contains a description of their role to be played (Refer to Role Play Situations). Role players also receive name tags. For each situation, the role players are asked to briefly leave the room to study their respective parts. They are asked to not converse with each other until the exercise begins. Each role player would receive instructions that might read as follows:
   "As you read your role description, take a few minutes to think about how you might feel if you were actually that person. Reflect silently without talking to others. On your name tag, write a new name for yourself for your role and wear the name tag during your role play. As soon as you have a good idea for your role, return to the room to begin."
3. While the role players are studying their parts, a description of the role playing situation can be given to the rest of the participants. These people can be invited to imagine how they might engage in their own portrayal of the parts.
4. When the role players are ready, they return to the room and are asked to enact the situation. The leader might allow the role plays to continue as long as productive interactions are taking place but not more than 10-15 minutes each, depending on total time allocated.

5. At the conclusion of the role play, the leader might remind the role players that it is useful to stay in role when initially discussing their feelings and responses to the role play.

Debriefing

Some Questions for the Role Players:

a. How do you feel in the role of _____?
b. What feelings do you have about the persons you've been interacting with?
c. What do you think they feel about you?

After assisting the role players in discussing their reactions, the leader instructs the role players to step out of role and join the rest of the students in a discussion of the role play exercise.

Some Questions for the "Class" Members:

a. What were you feeling during the role playing experience?
b. How might you have responded differently if you were in this situation? What other ways of responding can you think of?
c. If this situation were to occur in real life, what might the individuals need to handle the situation constructively?

Tips for Role Playing

Suggestions to Role Players:

Role playing exercises are structured to give you the opportunity to temporarily act like another person. Through role playing you are given the chance to try to "step into another person's shoes" and see the world from that person's perspective. You will be able to learn more from the experience if you wholeheartedly try to "become" that person as completely as you can. Here are some suggestions that you might follow:

1. Spend a few minutes thinking about the person whose role you are playing. Ask yourself: "How would I feel if I really were this person?" "How would I behave?" "How would I try to express myself?"
2. During the role play exercise, respond as spontaneously as you can.
3. You will be more effective as a role player if you are able to concentrate your attention just on the role players involved in your situation. Try to ignore the rest of the group.
4. Try to give your role play your best effort. "Clowning" around is not helpful.

Suggestions for Observers:

You can assist the role players by remaining silent during the role plays. Try to identify with one of the role players and feel what s/he might be feeling. Rather than judge the quality of the acting, try to imagine how you might respond if you were engaged in that role play.

Role-Play Situations

Situation 1: Parent and Child

Parent: Your eight-year-old child's pet dog, Muffy, has just been hit by an automobile and killed. Your child is arriving home from school and doesn't yet know that his/her dog has been killed.

Child: You are just arriving home from school. You are eight years old and are excited about going outside to play when you get home. You are also excited about telling your parents about how well you did in school today. As you walk through the door you notice that your dog, Muffy, is not around as he usually is. You call his name and ask where he is.

Situation 2: College Roommates

Roommate A: Your roommate is in class. You have just received a call from her father. He was very distraught and was trying to reach your roommate to tell her to come home immediately. He told you that her mother, who had been very ill, just died. He hangs up without specifically telling you whether you should be the one to tell your roommate that her mother is dead.

Roommate B: You are returning from Biology class to your room at college. You expect to see your roommate and to continue talking about your "big date" for the coming weekend. You are excited because this will be the first weekend in over a month that you will be at school. The last several weekends you have driven the 200 miles home to be with your mother who has been sick in the hospital. You are worried about her but have been assured by your mother and rest of your family that they'll call you if there's anything you can do.

Situation 3: Family Investment

Physician: You have recently completed diagnostic tests on a 20-year-old woman. Cancer has been discovered in the lower thigh of her right leg and it is necessary that her leg be amputated immediately in order to decrease the chances of cancer spreading. However, you know that there is a very strong chance that the cancer may have already spread, leaving your patient in danger for her life. Your patient is an outstanding ballet dancer who is currently dancing for the university dance troupe. Her lifelong aspiration has been to become a professional dancer.

Patient: You are a 20-year-old woman who is recognized as an outstanding ballet dancer. Currently you are dancing for the university dance troupe. You have always dreamed of becoming a professional ballet dancer. Four weeks ago you began to experience pain in your right leg. You assume that the pain in your leg is due to the strains from long hours of practice and are anxious to have it remedied so you can return to your full practice schedule.

Parent: You are the mother of a 20-year-old woman. You are accompanying your daughter to the physician to learn the results of her diagnostic tests. Your daughter is an outstanding ballet dancer. You are very proud of your daughter's success and you enthusiastically share her dream that she become a professional ballet dancer. Four weeks ago your daughter began experiencing pain in her right leg. At first, you were not concerned. But now you are very worried about the potential seriousness of your daughter's ailment. You feel compelled to find out everything you can from the physician about the diagnosis. You demand the physician give you concrete answers about the ailment, treatment, and the prognosis. You keep pushing until you feel you have all the facts.

Situation 4: Religious Issues

Friend A: Your best friend's father has been diagnosed with terminal cancer and is expected to die in a matter of weeks. You know that religious faith is very important to your friend and he firmly believes that his religious faith will somehow protect his father from dying.

Friend B: Your father has been diagnosed with terminal cancer. The physicians have told you and your family that your father is expected to die in just a matter of weeks. You have a deep conviction in your religious faith and firmly believe your faith will somehow protect your father from dying. You are with your best friend and you are curious about his religious views and ask him. Does he also believe in the power of your faith to protect your father from dying?

Situation 5: Attitudes of Helpers Toward Death

Physician (or other helper): Your patient has widespread cancer of the lung and it is anticipated she will die in a matter of weeks.

Patient: You know you have cancer of the lung. You are very frightened and ask "Am I going to die?" After s/he gives you an answer, you ask, "What will death be like? What would you feel, doctor, if you were me?"

Situation 6: Communication About Loss

Nurse: Your patient is a 29-year-old woman who is a very outgoing, energetic, vibrant person. You know that yesterday she was informed by the physician that her right breast would have to be surgically removed due to cancer. However, you also know that the patient was not informed about the full implications of her diagnosis. There seems to be clear indication that the cancer may have already spread. The prognosis for her is actually very poor with the likelihood that she may die very soon. You are visiting the patient to prepare her for surgery the following day. You know that your patient thinks that she will recover quickly after the operation. You wonder whether you should tell her the whole truth, or instead try to keep the patient's spirits up.

Patient: You are a 29-year-old woman who has always been highly energetic and outgoing. Several weeks ago, you discovered a lump in your breast. Yesterday, you were informed by your physician that your right breast would have to be removed immediately. Surgery is scheduled for tomorrow. You are in the hospital. A nurse that you feel comfortable with has just come in to see you. There are so many questions you would like to have answered, especially from another woman. Since you and your fiancee are planning to be married in three months, you ask the nurse whether she thinks he will still find you sexually appealing. Other questions: Will you be able to go swimming next summer? If so, what kind of bathing suit should you wear? Will you be able to play tennis? Go skiing? You ask the nurse how she might feel if she herself would have to lose her breast? You also ask the nurse what the risks of the operation really are?

Situation 7: Guilt

Friend A: Your friend's older brother was recently killed in an automobile accident. Since the accident your friend has talked incessantly about how guilty s/he feels. S/he states over and over again, "It should have been me that was killed, not my brother Jim." You care for your friend, a very great deal, and try to comfort her/him as best you can.

Friend B: Several weeks ago your older brother, Jim, was killed in an automobile accident. Since the accident you have been terribly distraught. Down deep inside you feel extremely guilty. On the day of the accident, you and Jim had had an argument over who was to get to use the car. He won the argument and took the car. At the time you were so angry you secretly wished he would "drop dead." Now, you feel so guilty that you wish it was you who died and not Jim. You are visiting with a good friend and you find yourself saying, "It should have been me that was killed."

Situation 8: "Right to Die"

Roommate A: You have recently returned to school after having visited your parents over the weekend. During your visit you had a serious discussion with your father about death and illness. Your father made a request: Should he ever be bedridden with a terminal disease, he wants you to make sure that no efforts are made to prolong his life through medication, or through any other means. He simply prefers to let the disease run its course and to die naturally. You told your father that you would need to think about his request before giving him an answer.

When you returned to school, you decided to talk to your roommate about this issue. You explain your situation to your roommate and then ask her/him what s/he might do if s/he were you. After you listen to her/his response, you try to explain how you feel.

Roommate B: Your roommate has recently returned after having visited with her/his parents. You can sense that something has been on her/his mind since the visit and you imagine that s/he might like to talk to you about it. You do your best to be available to her/him.

Situation 9: Loss

Friend A: Your best friend recently broke his leg on a skiing trip. He will be in a cast for several months. Prior to breaking his leg, he was an outstanding athlete who actively competed in basketball, baseball, and soccer. Since breaking his leg, he has seemed withdrawn and hard to talk to. You wonder what is going on with him and ask him.

Friend B: Recently you broke your leg on a skiing trip and will be in a cast for several months. The physicians have hinted that you might not regain full use of your leg because it was a serious break. Prior to your accident, you were an outstanding athlete who competed in basketball, baseball, and soccer. Often, you even dream of becoming a professional athlete. Now, although you've never told anyone, you are afraid you might never be able to run again. Lately, you've been spending more and more time alone because it's hard for you to see your friends being active and having fun. Sometimes, you just want to scream out how unfair it is. Sometimes, it makes you furious to see how much your friends take their health for granted and you find yourself secretly asking, "Why me and not them?" One of your best friends has just dropped by to see you. Suddenly, during your conversation, you blurt out how frustrated and angry you are.

V. Additional Considerations

This is not truly a fifth category of fully outlined SLEs, but the manual would be incomplete without mention of the best sources of writing useful for reflecting on life and death. We firmly believe that good literature with death and loss themes offers the best source of death education "material," as it provides context and the richness of variety that only the growing number of available sources of such reading at all developmental levels can now afford.

Brief works of fiction, in particular, seem to hold special opportunities for rich learning and powerful contemplation and identification by the reader. One source of these is found in Rose Somerville's edited collection titled *Intimate Relationships: Marriage, Family and Lifestyles Through Literature* (Englewood Cliffs, NJ: Prentice Hall 1975). Section IV (pp. 259-370) of this book is a fine collection of eight short pieces with varied loss and death themes.

Another good compendium of literary shorts germane to the topic is the previously cited (Introduction), *We Are But A Moment's Sunlight* edited by Adler, Stanford, and Adler. And, the best sourcebooks for this and other thanatological materials are these: Joanne Bernstein's *Books to Help Children Cope With Separation and Loss* (New York: Bowker, 1977) — not all of which are necessarily limited for very young audiences. And, Wass, et al's *Death Education: An Annotated Resource Guide* (Washington: Hemisphere, 1980). The latter is a collection of diverse references and annotations for use in death education.

Hereafter we've listed a few mini-exercises which are appropriate for adolescents and older participants, and which serve to illustrate the point made above. Included are some titles, authors, main goals, procedural suggestions, and a short set of debriefing outlines for each.

These are just some of many excellent literary works, mostly short stories, which lend themselves marvelously to a reflective learning experience in death education. The reader is encouraged to investigate the sources available for finding more of their genre, and to devise creative ways to compare such works or to use them in facilitating attitude formation with students.

Finally, the field of death education itself has grown steadily of late, and there are numerous, very helpful recent publications with which to augment the classroom or workshop experience. While it's not the intent of this volume to catalog these, we strongly recommend a careful selection from among them as primary reading material for learning more about the contemporary matters of living in the face of human mortality.

50a. Day of the Last Rock Fight
by Joseph Whitehall

Goal

To promote evaluation of loyalty, friendship, revenge and motivation as they relate to death.

Procedures

When assigning this story, it helps to make readers aware in advance that this is a story written in the 1950s as a letter from a boy to his father.

Debriefing

1. What is sufficient motivation for murder?
2. What is sufficient motivation for suicide?
3. How can families support a member who is directly or indirectly involved in the death of a peer?
4. Is mental illness avoidance of responsibility when involved in a death experience?
5. Do public, institutional compulsory mourning rituals generate or exacerbate guilt when a peer dies?
6. Is the deliberate premeditated death of Gene different from Peter's suicide?

50b. A Death in the Family by James Agee*
The Death of Ivan Illich
by Leo Tolstoy

Goal To compare grief and death behavior in these two classic short stories.

Procedures

Ask them to note any similarities or differences in grief and death behaviors while reading. Have each participant choose a particularly memorable passage and later share those and identify similarities or differences noted.

Debriefing

1. How are the readings alike? Different?
2. Compare them in relation to acceptance and denial of death by the characters.
3. Are they "accurate" presentations of loss and grief sequelae?
4. Which story did you like better? Why? Which is closer to your view of death, loss or grief?
5. How was each universal in its treatment of this theme or topic?
6. How was each culturally or historically unique?
7. Which character(s) did you most identify with? Why?

---

*Suggested by Pat Hess, San Francisco, CA.

50c.   Scarlet Ibis by James Hurst

Goals

1. To examine the quality of life and relationships in a family with a handicapped child.
2. To examine beliefs about symbols of life and death.
3. To explore guilt and responsibility in childhood experiences of death.

Procedures

Assign a reading of the story and debrief soon thereafter.

Debriefing

1. Did you like it? How did you feel about this story?
2. What symbols of life and death were in the story? Were there any that symbolized both?
3. Should Doodle have died when he was born? When he did?
4. Did his brother cause his death?
5. What might Doodle's life have been like without his brother?
6. How are love and hate and life and death connected?
7. How are guilt and death related to one another?
8. Is guilt part of the mourning process?
9. How does the impending threat of death of a family member effect a family?

50d.   Occurrence at Owl Creek Bridge and Chickamauga by Ambrose Bierce

Goals

1. To compare two works set in the same time period but with different views of death.
2. To compare child and adult views of death in war.

Procedures

These two works are also available as short films and can be shown or assigned for reading.

Debriefing

1. In what ways were the presentations of death similar?
2. How was the child's view of death realistic in terms of developmental level?
3. How was the adult view presented?
4. How did each view life while participating in a death situation?
5. Does sudden violent death heighten survivors' awareness of life?

About the Authors

The editors (and original authors of most of these exercises) are all experienced educators and clinicians.

J. Eugene Knott, Ph.D., is a counseling psychologist, administrator, and faculty member at the University of Rhode Island and has published numerous papers in the field, and who is past-president of the Forum for Death Education and Counseling. *Mary C. Ribar, M.A.*, is chairperson of the English Department and Interdisciplinary Team Leader at a public school in Montgomery County, Maryland; Ms. Ribar is a creative teacher of wide-ranging experience, and has presented at numerous thanatology conferences. *Betty M. Duson, Ph.D.* and *Marc R. King, Ph.D.* are both clinical psychologists and experienced therapists and teachers in the field. She was formerly Director of Training at the Counseling Center at the University of Houston, and is now in private practice as a psychotherapist in Houston, while he is presently on the staff of both the counseling and psychology departments at Southern Methodist University in Dallas, Texas. Both have been creating and refining SLEs for several years as college and graduate level instructors at two other universities.

Index